# The Strange World of Sea Mammals

## *About the Book*

Many creatures that dwell in the seas cannot live without rising periodically to the surface to breathe. Some air-breathing sea creatures can come ashore for long periods and be as much at home as they are in the deeps. Others cannot survive ashore any better than they would survive at sea without surfacing for air. Here is the illustrated story of the origins of sea mammals, their life cycles, their environment, and their constant peril in a world dominated by *homo sapiens*.

Ross seal
(*Ommatophoca rossi*)

Amphibians—frogs
and tadpoles

North Alaskan eskimo
harpooning a bowhead
whale from an umiak

# The Strange World of

# Sea Mammals

by William Wise

Illustrated by

Joseph Sibal

G. P. Putnam's Sons · New York

*To Philip and Lucy*

Baikal seal
(*Pusa sibirica*)

SBN: GB-399-60793-5
TR-399-20306-0
*Library of Congress Catalog Card Number: 72-83334*
PRINTED IN THE UNITED STATES OF AMERICA
12216

Blackfish or pilot whale
(*Globicephala melaena*)

Egg-laying mammal
Duckbill platypus
(*Ornithorhynchus anatinus*)

# Contents

White shark
(*Carcharodon carcharias*)

Dolphins chasing flying fish
(*Cypselurus californicus*)

Steller's sea cow
(*Hydrodamalis stelleri*)

# 1
# A Vanished Giant

Steller's sea cow with baby

IN 1741 a small, creaky wooden ship, the *St. Peter*, under the command of Captain Vitus Bering, sailed from a port in Siberia to explore the northern Pacific Ocean and the coast of Alaska. Aboard was a German naturalist, George Wilhelm Steller. The dangerous voyage lasted two years, and by the time it was done Steller had discovered a remarkable sea animal no trained observer ever had seen before — or ever would see again.

Steller only made his discovery after a number of misfortunes had occurred. First the expedition ran out of fresh fruit and vegetables, and the men fell sick with scurvy. Several died. Then storms drove the *St. Peter* hundreds of miles off course. Finally, to obtain drinking water and to regain their strength, Steller and the others decided to remain for a time on one of the barren Commander Islands. Here another storm hurled their ship onto the beach, a badly damaged wreck.

It was then, as they lived in huts and dugouts on Copper Island and tried to repair their ship, that Steller noticed three different kinds of animals in the vicinity. Ashore there were blue foxes so tame that they came up to the sailors and sniffed and snapped at them. There were thousands of sea otters offshore, floating in thick beds of kelp. Also in the water, and especially noticeable at high tide, were a number of strange-looking, humpbacked creatures. From a distance these huge, slow-swimming animals resembled nothing so much as long, overturned boats. Gradually Steller came to realize that they were sea cows, but a giant species never previously observed.

7

Colony of sea otters (*Enhydra lutris*)

Even while living in miserable conditions on the beach, the German naturalist somehow managed to keep a journal. In it he wrote the only expert, eyewitness account we shall ever have of the northern — Steller's — sea cow, the unique sea-dwelling mammal that still bears his name. In part this is what Steller wrote:

These animals love shallow and sandy places along the seashore, but they spend their time more particularly about the mouths of the gullies and brooks, the rushing water of which always attracts them in herds. They keep the half-grown and young in front of them when pasturing, and are very careful to guard them in the middle of the herd. With the rising tide they

8

come in so close to the shore that not only did I on many occasions prod them with a pole or spear, but sometimes even stroked their backs with my hand. . . . Usually entire families keep together, the male and the female, one grown offspring and a little tender one. . . .

In another entry Steller described the way these giant sea mammals fed on the abundant seaweed offshore. While eating, he wrote, they

lift the nostrils every four or five minutes out of the water, blowing out air and a little water with a noise like that of a horse snorting. While browsing they move slowly forward, one foot after another, and in this manner, half swim, half walk like cattle or sheep grazing. Half the body is always out of the water. Gulls are in the habit of sitting on the backs of the feeding animals, feasting on the vermin infesting the skin as crows are wont to do on the lice of hogs and sheep. . . .

Steller and the other explorers were desperate for food. Before they had finished repairing their ship they killed and ate several of the gentle, browsing animals. Then they relaunched the *St. Peter* and sailed back to Siberia. On their return — and without intending to — they brought about the destruction of the last 4,000 or 5,000 giant sea cows left in the world.

Steller and the others did this by selling the furs of the blue foxes and of the several hundred sea otters they had killed for food during their eight months on Copper Island. Word soon spread that valuable pelts could be obtained in the Commanders. Before long both Copper and Bering islands were overrun with hunting parties. Naturally, the hunters had to eat, and they found the giant sea cows pleasant tasting and easy to kill. In less than twenty years the sea cows were gone from Copper Island, and only a handful — the last of all — were left around Bering Island.

An attempt was made to save the few remaining herds. In what may have been mankind's first effort to safeguard an endangered species of wildlife, a Russian engineer named Peter Jakovlev asked the Siberian authorities to protect the giant sea cows from their persecutors. His pleas went unheeded. The hunting continued, and about 150 or 200 years ago (some authorities say only 27 years after Steller's discovery) the last animals were killed.

Today, in addition to Steller's journal, we have only a few pieces of skin and some other anatomical exhibits preserved in one or two of our museums to tell us what the giant sea cows were like. In all of the

Blue foxes (*Alopex lagopus pribilofensis*)

northern seas not a single animal now wallows offshore, guarding its young, feeding on sea vegetation, drifting back and forth with the tide.

The northern sea cow was but one of many sea mammals that men have hunted ruthlessly during the past several centuries. The extinction of Steller's harmless giant was really only an early chapter in a story of greedy slaughter and careless, often senseless destruction that continues to the present day.

How the story will close we do not yet know. All anyone can say is that within the next years, for better or worse, the last chapters will be written. Which sea mammals will be left by then it is difficult to guess.

# 2
# The Animals Divided

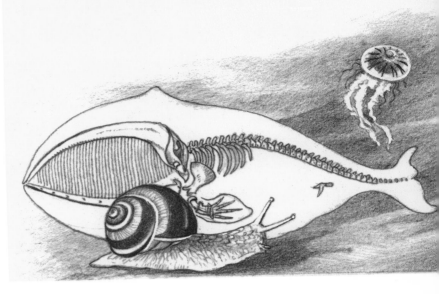

Vertebrate—Whale
Invertebrate—Snail
and jellyfish

EXACTLY WHAT SORT of animal was the huge sea cow of the northern Pacific Ocean? When we say it was a sea-dwelling mammal, what do we mean? In the scheme of living things, where did Steller's inoffensive, vanished giant actually belong?

The answer to these questions can be understood best if we first examine the way zoologists classify different kinds of animals. To begin with, all animals now are classified by their anatomy — that is, by the way they are built. Zoologists have agreed there are two principal types of animals: those with backbones, and those without. Animals with backbones are called vertebrates, while animals without are called invertebrates. A vertebra is a bone, or a segment of cartilage, that forms part of an animal's spinal column.

On land there are many kinds of invertebrate animals. Spiders, cockroaches, wasps, worms — none have backbones. In the water there are numerous invertebrates too. Clams and oysters do not have backbones. Neither do snails, crabs, jellyfish, or squids.

Most of the creatures that we usually think of as animals, though, do have backbones. Some, like sea turtles and fish, live in the water. Others, like dogs and cats or cows and horses, live on land. Sometimes, when we are not being scientific, we say that the vertebrates are "higher" animals; what we chiefly mean is that their anatomies are more complicated than those of the invertebrates.

Among the vertebrate animals there are five main classes. The earliest to develop were the fishes. Hundreds of millions of years ago they began to live in the warm, shallow seas that covered much of the world. Since then they have changed comparatively little. Today fish still live in the water and obtain oxygen through gills rather than

11

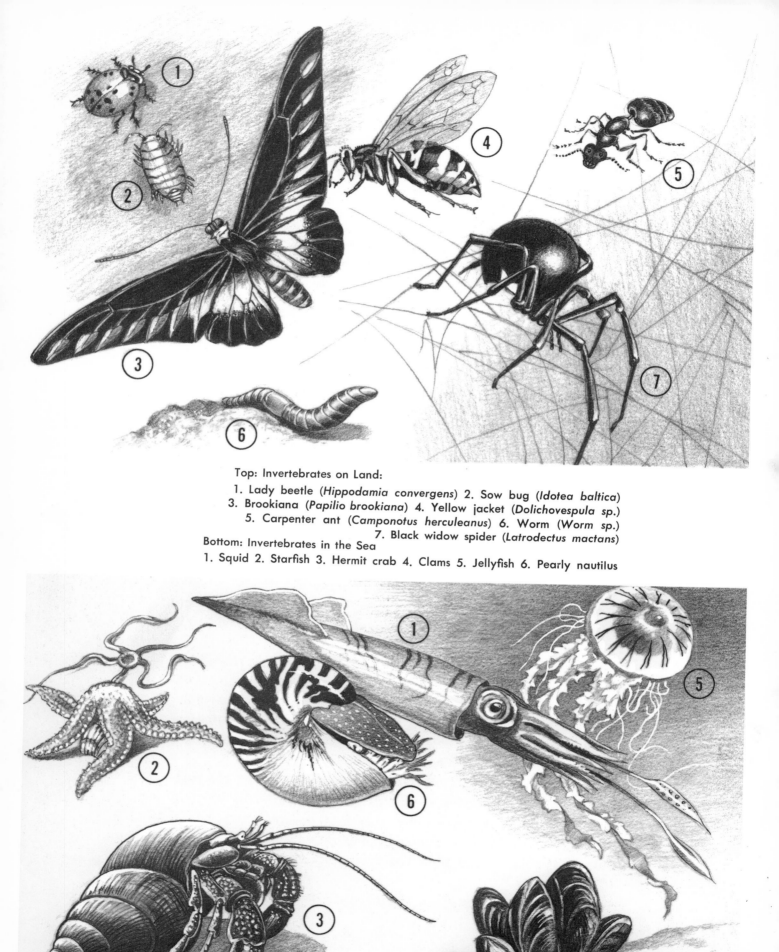

Top: Invertebrates on Land:

1. Lady beetle (*Hippodamia convergens*) 2. Sow bug (*Idotea baltica*)
3. Brookiana (*Papilio brookiana*) 4. Yellow jacket (*Dolichovespula sp.*)
5. Carpenter ant (*Camponotus herculeanus*) 6. Worm (*Worm sp.*)
7. Black widow spider (*Latrodectus mactans*)

Bottom: Invertebrates in the Sea

1. Squid 2. Starfish 3. Hermit crab 4. Clams 5. Jellyfish 6. Pearly nautilus

lungs. Most fish still reproduce their young by laying eggs. And they are cold-blooded animals. This means that the temperature of their bodies will rise when their surroundings grow warmer and will fall when their surroundings grow colder.

After millions of years a second class of cold-blooded vertebrate animals began to appear. These were the amphibians — animals that live both in the water and on land.

The first amphibians probably developed from fish that learned to come ashore briefly, either to feed or to travel to nearby bodies of water. Today the best-known amphibians are frogs and toads. In the water, young frogs, or tadpoles, breathe through their gills, like their distant fish ancestors. But once they change into adult frogs, they breathe only through their lungs.

The third class of vertebrate animals to develop were the reptiles. Like fish and amphibians, the reptiles also were cold-blooded animals. In the sun their bodies grew warmer, and in the shade their bodies grew colder. But unlike their amphibian forebears, the reptiles had no gills. They had lungs and were exclusively air-breathing animals, as they are today.

For millions of years the early reptiles were supreme, both on land and in the water and air. The land reptiles were the dinosaurs. Those reptiles that lived in the warm seas, though they breathed air, were the ichthyosaurs and plesiosaurs. And the flying reptiles were what we call pterosaurs.

Vertebrates in the Sea
1. Marlin (*Makaira albida*) 2. Tiger shark (*Galeocerdo cuvieri*) 3. Loggerhead turtle (*Eretmochelys imbricata*) 4. Pilot fish (*Naucrates ductor*)

Prehistoric
reptiles on land
—Dinosaurs
1. Tyrannosaurus
2. Torosaurus
3. Nyctosaurus
4. Cetiosaurus
5. Edaphosaurus

About 60,000,000 or 70,000,000 years ago the last of these fantastic animals died off. Other reptiles, though, have continued to live in the world down to our own day. At present there are four groups of reptiles. They are the snakes, the crocodiles, the turtles, and the lizards. Like their ancient and spectacular ancestors, all of today's reptiles are cold-blooded, air-breathing animals.

During the millions of years that the reptiles ruled the world the last two classes of vertebrate animals — the birds and the mammals — slowly began to develop. About 150,000,000 years ago, while the grotesque pterosaurs still were flying through the air, a small but important creature appeared in the trees. This was *Archaeopteryx*, the ancestor of every one of the birds we see today.

*Archaeopteryx* was really half reptile and half bird. It had claws on its wings; it probably had reptilelike scales on its head; and it had a mouthful of teeth — a most unbirdlike characteristic.

Yet *Archaeopteryx* was certainly not a reptile. It had feathers, and it was a warm-blooded animal. All of today's birds, unlike reptiles, amphibians, or fish, are warm-blooded too. Their bodies maintain a

14

constant temperature, whether the surrounding air turns warmer or colder.

The other class of vertebrate animals that emerged were the mammals. At roughly the same time that *Archaeopteryx* and its descendants were developing into birds, a number of reptilelike animals were changing in a new direction. One was a mammallike reptile called *Cynognathus*, a name which means dog-jawed. Very little is known about this curious animal. But zoologists believe that today's mammals, including man, probably developed from *Cynognathus* or from one of its close relatives.

Over a period of millions of years a great variety of different mammals have appeared on earth. The descendants of many of them are still alive; often they do not seem to resemble one another in any way at all. As a result, it is not always easy to define a mammal or to state precisely what one is.

Zoologists do agree, however, on several points. All mammals, the experts say, feed their young with milk produced in their bodies; all mammals have hearts with four chambers; and with the exception of

Prehistoric reptiles
in the sea
1. Stenopterygius
2. Ophthalmosaurus
3. Kronosaurus
4. Pteranodon
5. Macroplata
1 & 2 Ichthyosaurs
3 & 5 Plesiosaurs
4 Pterosaurs

15

Orders of sea mammals

1. Cetacea—Whales

2. Sirenia—Manatees

3. Carnivora—Sea otters

4. Pinnipedia—Seals

certain kinds of whales, all mammals have at least a few hairs on their bodies. Also, mammals are warm-blooded and breathe air through their lungs. In addition, all mammals except two — the spiny anteater and the duckbill platypus — give birth to living young, instead of laying eggs like all birds and like the majority of fish and reptiles.

The earliest mammals lived on land; most mammals have continued to do so ever since. But at different times a few kinds returned to the sea — to the place where animal life had first developed. In order to make this return successfully, each mammal was forced to adapt in its own way to an environment that it was unaccustomed to. The process must have taken hundreds of thousands or in some cases, millions of years. During this time, legs became flippers, disappeared entirely, or changed into tails; bodies became streamlined, as an aid to swimming; a layer of fat, or blubber, was developed beneath the skin to keep the animal warm and buoyant even in the iciest seas.

Today some sea mammals have changed so much that they cannot return to land; they are helpless there. Other sea mammals have changed less; although they remain at sea most of the year, they return to shore during the breeding season to mate and give birth to their young.

There are now about 4,200 kinds, or species, of land mammals in the world. But there are only 136 species of mammals that live entirely or mostly in the water. There are two large families, or orders, of sea mammals. One order consists of the whales, or Cetacea; the other of

17

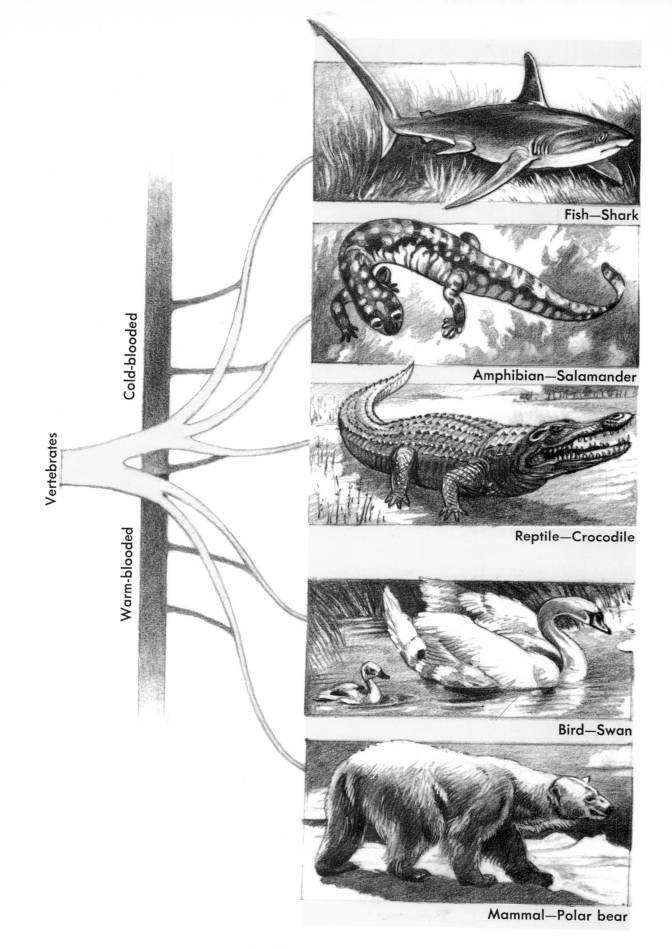

Fish—Shark

Amphibian—Salamander

Reptile—Crocodile

Bird—Swan

Mammal—Polar bear

Cold-blooded

Warm-blooded

Vertebrates

Classification of vertebrates

the seals, or Pinnipedia. There also are the sea otters, a part of the order Carnivora; and there is another small order called Sirenia, to which Steller's sea cow ( *Hydrodamalis stelleri* ) belongs.

The sea mammals in one family often tend to be quite unlike those in another; yet, despite their differences, all sea mammals have certain characteristics in common. Perhaps the most important one they share is this: At different times, and in different ways, each kind of sea mammal returned to the water and adapted itself to a new and difficult environment. And there it has lived, often with great success, for millions of years, until the recent appearance of a new and deadly adversary — modern man.

Probable sources of tales of sea serpents:
Top, South American rat snake
(Ptyas pantherinus)
Center, Conger eel (Conger oceanicus)
Bottom, Sea snake (Hydrus bicolor)

# 3
# The
# Sea Serpent
# and
# the Kraken

A kraken

For thousands of years people lived in awe of the sea. In every age voyagers dreaded the storms that might spring up suddenly and swamp their ships; and they feared sailing into unmapped waters, where hidden rocks or shoals could bring death to everyone aboard.

But perhaps most terrifying of all were the strange animals that were said to live in the ocean. People everywhere believed in monsters of the deep. Hadn't they listened to spectacular firsthand accounts of seafaring men? And in the case of sailors themselves, hadn't they, on a misty day, or just before dusk, caught glimpses of sinister, mysterious shapes floating half concealed beneath the surface of the water?

Stories of ocean monsters — of sirens and mermaids, sea serpents and krakens — have persisted in every age down to our own. Yet the curious thing is that a certain amount of truth probably lies behind all but the most fanciful of these tales and legends. Often a reported "monster" was only an inoffensive sea animal seen through the fearful eyes of a superstitious traveler. Often, too, it was one of the sea mammals that was mistaken for a supposedly dangerous or magical beast.

Tales of giant sea serpents were repeated by the most sober and intelligent men. In ancient Greece, Aristotle wrote of sea-dwelling monsters during the fourth century B.C. "The serpents in Libya," he informed his readers, "are very large. Mariners sailing along the coast have told how they have seen the bones of many oxen which, it was apparent to them, have been devoured by the serpents. And as their ship sailed on, the serpents came and attacked them, some of them throwing themselves onto the trireme and capsizing it."

21

Pliny the Elder was a Roman writer of military history. A common-sense ex-cavalry officer, he nevertheless believed in sea monsters too. In one book he reported that a squadron of Greek ships sent to the Persian Gulf by Alexander the Great had been attacked by "sea serpents thirty feet long."

These early stories probably grew out of two main sources. They came from travelers' descriptions of huge land snakes, like the African and Indian python, that attain a length of more than 20 feet when mature; and they came from fishermen's yarns about conger eels and the small but poisonous snakes which are to be found in some of the tropical oceans.

Two thousand years and more after Pliny and Aristotle many people in Europe and America still believed in sea serpents. And from time to time there would be a new "discovery" that seemed to confirm the existence of these dangerous monsters.

One such discovery occurred less than 200 years ago, in the Orkney Islands, off the northern coast of Scotland. Here in 1808, on some sunken rocks near the island of Stronsay, the partially decomposed carcass of a giant sea animal was found by a party of fishermen. Local residents went to inspect it. They never had seen anything remotely like the creature. Could it possibly be a genuine sea serpent?

Excitement rose to feverish heights on Stronsay. The monster was described by sworn witnesses; measurements and drawings were made of the carcass; a part of the skull and spine were carefully packed and shipped to Edinburgh University, where a number of professors examined them. Soon the most eminent among them declared that in his opinion the specimen found on Stronsay was a unique animal previ-

African python
(*Python sebae*)

ously unknown to science. In fact, it was undoubtedly an example of that much sought-after and elusive beast, the sea serpent!

In London a famous surgeon and anatomist read a newspaper account of this extraordinary discovery. His curiosity was aroused. He wrote to Edinburgh and asked for a portion of the skeleton. He received two of the vertebrae; after studying them, he announced his findings. Unfortunately for the lovers of romantic tales, the Stronsay sea serpent was no such thing. It was merely a large example of a real giant of the deep—*Cetorhinus maximus*, the basking shark.

Some thirty-seven years later a great number of huge animal bones were found in Alabama. They were the fossil remains of a long-extinct primitive whale called *Basilosaurus* or *Zeuglodon*. These bones fell into the hands of an enterprising charlatan, "Dr." Albert Koch. Before long Dr. Koch had taken the bones, added numerous plaster vertebrae to lengthen the skeleton, and declared that he had discovered the remains of an ancient 114-foot sea serpent.

Dr. Koch took the skeleton to Europe and went from capital to capital charging admissions. Eventually he sold his prize to the King of Prussia in exchange for an annual pension. The king gave the skeleton to the Berlin Museum, where experts examined it and shortened it to 75 feet.

In the meantime Dr. Koch had returned to the United States, and there he built himself a second sea serpent skeleton. He again toured Europe, exhibiting it successfully in Prague, Vienna, and Berlin. Finally he sold the skeleton to the Wood's Museum in Chicago. Here a gullible public continued to pay money to gape at it, until it was destroyed in the famous fire of 1871.

Even now, in our own century, the myth of the sea serpent refuses to die. During the summer of 1933 the Loch Ness monster was first observed in a large lake in Scotland. By autumn it had become famous all over the world. Newspapermen came from as far away as Tokyo in the hope of catching a glimpse of the creature. A circus operator said he would pay $100,000 to anyone who could deliver it to him alive. The New York Zoological Society offered $20,000 for it.

But the Loch Ness monster proved hard to capture. In fact, the Scottish sea serpent has avoided its pursuers to this day. No one has succeeded in bringing it ashore; no one even has managed to take a single convincing photograph of "Nessie," which is her current newspaper name. Visitors to the remote lake, however, still report sighting the mysterious animal from time to time, often on rainy days or just before nightfall, when the light is poor. And scientific investigations

Basking shark (*Cetorhinus maximus*) (Inset, basking attitude)

continue to be made in the hope of determining whether or not a large marine animal actually does live in the depths of the lake. What these efforts may eventually disclose it is impossible to say. A current theory is that Nessie might be a mother otter and her family of pups, the latter swimming after her, single file, through the water.

One early description of the Loch Ness monster, though, strongly suggests a different explanation. The report was made by a vacationing couple who drove by the lake during the summer of 1933. To their astonishment, a large animal began to cross the road ahead of their car. It had a thick body, no legs, and a long neck that undulated up and down, "in the manner of a scenic railway train." The couple said the animal's body was gray, like a rhinoceros or a dirty elephant, and that it moved in a series of jerks.

This report suggests that the original Loch Ness monster was a seal, probably a large specimen of the harbor seal (*Phoca vitulina*), which is frequently sighted in the waters around Scotland. In all likelihood, it had swum in from the open sea, up the River Ness, and then into the lake. And one day, after becoming a universally recognized personality, it probably returned to sea by the same route.

24

According to popular legend, the most gigantic marine monster of all was the kraken. This huge creature was encountered by sailors in various northern seas but particularly near Norway, in the polar ocean.

Two hundred years ago Erik Pontopiddan, writing in his *Natural History of Norway*, said of the kraken, "Amongst the many great things which are in the ocean, and concealed from our eyes, or only present to our view for a few minutes, is the Kraken. This creature is the largest and most surprising of all animal creation. . . ."

The writer went on to say that a fair-sized adult kraken might run to "a mile and a half in circumference." Sometimes sailors mistook it for an island, landed on its back, and lit a fire to cook their supper. After a while the kraken felt the heat of the fire and plunged down into the sea, with fatal results for the sailors who had been eating or sleeping around the campfire.

There never was much agreement among experts concerning the kraken's disposition. Some said it was gentle and harmless, despite its colossal size. Others claimed that it was a fierce, aggressive animal.

Pontopiddan's description of a surfacing kraken leaves little doubt what it really was. "At last," he wrote, "several bright points appear, which grow thicker and thicker, the higher they rise above the surface of the water, and sometimes stand as high and as large as the masts of

A prehistoric cetacean—*Basilosaurus*, or *Zeuglodon*

Indian python (*Python molurus*)

middle-size vessels. It seems these are the creature's arms, and it is said, if they were to lay hold of the largest warship, they would pull it to the bottom. . . ."

The monster described by Pontopiddan and other writers was undoubtedly a giant squid (*Architeuthis princeps*), a member of a class of animals called cephalopods. Giant squids grow to incredible size. They can be 50 or 60 feet in length and are the world's largest invertebrate animals.

Usually giant squids are only found in the deepest ocean waters. Occasionally, though, they will rise to the surface without warning. They are the favorite food of the sperm whale (*Physeter catodon*). The death struggle between a giant squid and one of these huge cetaceans is truly titanic; probably such battles were observed by early whalers and other seamen, and in time they contributed to some of the more fantastic stories about the mythical kraken.

# 4
# Mermaids, Sirens, and Sea Cows

Stories of sirens and mermaids were first told thousands of years ago. Since then, these lovely but dangerous creatures — half woman and half fish — have supposedly been seen in hundreds of different locations, from the Spice Islands of the Pacific to the icy coasts of Scandinavia and northern Canada.

In the earliest legends sirens and mermaids were always beautiful. Sometimes they carried a mirror, into which they idly gazed. More often, as they rode between the waves, they were supposed to run a comb through their long and charming sea-green hair.

A mermaid might be accompanied by her husband, a merman, who was half man and half fish. But sirens, at least originally, had no male companions. The sirens of the ancient Greeks were cruel sea nymphs; they sang beautiful songs and lured sailors to their doom on the rocks which surrounded the Mediterranean island where they lived.

Pliny the Elder had no doubts concerning the reality and appearance of mermaids. In a seventeenth-century translation of his *Natural History*, he is quoted as saying:

> It is no fabulous tale that is told of them; for look how painters draw them — so they are indeed; only their body is rough and scaled all over, even in those parts where they resemble a woman. For such a mermaid was seen . . . upon a coast near the shore; and the inhabitants dwelling there heard it far off when it was dying, to make piteous moans, crying and chattering very loudly.

Henry Hudson, the famous navigator, did not question that two members of his crew had seen a mermaid as their ship searched for the fabled Northwest Passage between the Atlantic and Pacific oceans. The incident occurred early in the 1600's in the Barents Sea, within the Arctic Circle, near the island of Novaya Zemlya.

This evening [Hudson wrote] one of our company, looking overboard, saw a mermaid, and called up some of the company to see her; one more of the crew came up, and by that time she was come close to the ship's side, looking earnestly at the men. A little after, the sea came and overturned her. From the navel upward her back and breasts were like a woman's, as they say that saw her; her body was as big as one of us, her skin very white, and long hair hanging down behind, of a color black. In her going down they saw her tail, which was like the tail of a porpoise, speckled like a mackerel.

Later in the same century several mermaids were reported thousands of miles away, in various tropical regions of the Pacific Ocean. One Dutch account said:

. . . in the year 1652 or 1653, a lieutenant in the service of the Company saw two of these beings in the gulf, near the village of Hennetelo, in the administrative district of Amboina. They were swimming side by side, which made him presume that one was male, the other female. Six weeks after, they reappeared in the same spot, and were seen by more than fifty persons. These monsters were of greenish gray color, having precisely the shape of human beings from the head to the waist, with arms and hands, but their bodies tapered away.

By a century or two ago most scientists had grown extremely skeptical of the existence of sirens and mermaids, although they were not yet able to identify for certain the real animals behind the legends. But at least a part of the general public continued to believe in these mythological creatures for a while longer, retaining their superstitious faith until almost our own day.

In 1808 a mermaid was seen off the coast of Scotland by a young lady named MacKay. She observed the mermaid swimming off the rocks. It had a face that was "round and plump, and of a bright pink hue." Miss MacKay did not actually see the mermaid gaze into a mirror, but every once in a while the sea creature "lifted a white arm and threw back some of her long green hair."

Later the same summer a schoolteacher named William Munro wrote a letter to the *Times* of London. In it he described a similar experience of his own, which also had taken place in Scotland.

Mr. Munro was walking by the shore. "My attention," he wrote, "was arrested by the appearance of a figure resembling an unclothed human female, sitting upon a rock extending into the sea. . . . The forehead was round, the face plump, the cheeks ruddy, the eyes blue, the mouth and lips of a natural form, resembling those of a man; the teeth I could not discover, as the mouth was shut. . . . the fingers from the action in which the hands were employed, did not appear to be webbed, but as to this I am not positive. It remained on the rock three or four minutes after I observed it, and was exercised in that period in combing its hair, which was long and thick, and of which it appeared proud, and then dropped into the sea, whence it did not reappear to me."

As our knowledge of ocean life has increased during the past few decades, the ancient belief in mermaids and sirens finally has died away. Today zoologists tell us that two kinds of sea mammals were probably responsible for most of the legends. One kind were members of the order Pinnipedia, the seals; no other animals, for instance, so closely fit the descriptions given by Henry Hudson's crewmen or by the schoolteacher William Munro. And seals frequently are seen in the northern regions of Scotland and in the Barents Sea, around Novaya Zemlya.

The second kind of sea mammals involved in the legends were members of the order Sirenia, a term derived from the word "siren." Three distinct types of animal belonging to this limited and highly specialized order have survived into recent times. One was Steller's sea cow. This huge, ungainly animal had nothing to do with sirens, however, for it could never have been mistaken for anything so small. An adult specimen was 25 or 30 feet long, or four to five times the length of a man or woman. Even at a distance it would have been impossible to confuse the giant sea cow with a quasi-human being. And the animal's habitat was so restricted that for hundreds of years it probably was seen only by local Eskimos.

The other and surviving members of Sirenia are the manatee and the dugong. Undoubtedly they often were sighted in southern waters by superstitious sailors; and from these encounters, particularly those involving dugongs, most stories about sirens apparently evolved.

The animal order Sirenia is a very old one. Fossil remains have been found which indicate that early members of the order were present in the warm, shallow seas of the Eocene period, at least 50,000,000 years ago, and perhaps even earlier. Unlikely as it seems, these sea animals apparently were closely related structurally to some of the strange-looking elephants that once lived on land. Many zoologists now believe that both the dugongs and manatees, as well as the modern elephant, are descendants of a common ancestor.

Manatees and dugongs have adapted completely to ocean and river life. They are almost totally helpless ashore, and if they become stranded, they cannot move their bodies enough to return to the water.

The manatee family consists of three species. The American manatee (*Trichechus manatus*) is usually between 8 and 12 feet long. It is found along the Atlantic coast of the United States, from North Carolina to Florida and the Gulf of Mexico. Manatees are protected in

Common ancestry,
top to bottom:
Manatee
Elephant
Dugong
Steller's sea cow

Dugong (*Dugong dugon*)

Florida. They often are seen in the Everglades and sometimes even appear within the city limits of Miami. The American manatee is also found farther south, through the West Indies, and along the western shore of the Caribbean Sea, from Vera Cruz southward as far as northeastern South America.

A second, slightly smaller species, the Amazonian manatee (*Trichechus inunguis*), lives only in fresh water. It can be found in the various rivers that make up the vast drainage systems of the Amazon and Orinoco rivers in South America. The third species (*Trichechus senegalensis*) lives on the other side of the Atlantic Ocean near the coast of West Africa, from Senegal to Angola. It spends most of its time at sea but sometimes enters fresh or brackish water, especially in the rivers that drain Lake Chad.

Manatees have two front flippers and a rounded tail. The young use only their flippers in swimming. Adults, though, use their tails for swimming, while they turn themselves to right or left with a deft use of their flippers.

31

The body of a manatee is rounded, its head is proportionately small, and it has a square snout. When wet, its skin is gray, but as the skin dries, it turns almost white. The manatee's nostrils are at the tip of its muzzle. It has no external ears. Thick hairs grow on its upper lip, and short hairs appear singly over much of its otherwise bare skin.

Observers report that manatees usually are seen swimming by themselves or in small family groups. Occasionally, however, they also congregate in larger numbers. As many as fifteen or twenty half-grown manatees have been seen together during cold weather migrating toward warmer waters.

Manatees can remain submerged for at least fifteen minutes and possibly longer. But usually they return to the surface at five- or ten-minute intervals, take a breath or two, and then submerge again. They are sluggish animals and often rest at the surface, with their backs arched and their tails well below the level of their heads. In shallow water they can rest on their tails if they choose; now and again they seem to enjoy "walking" on their flippers.

American manatee
(*Trichechus manatus*)

Amazonian manatee
(*Trichechus inunguis*)

When manatees meet, they may greet one another by rubbing their muzzles together. They are inquisitive animals and sometimes rise near a fisherman's boat to inspect the scene. Because they are nearsighted, they may come quite close. For people unfamiliar with the habits of manatees, their sudden emergence can be unnerving.

Although they are known to be active at almost any hour, manatees seem to feed mostly at night. They are entirely herbivorous and devour large amounts of marine, brackish, and freshwater plants and any terrestrial plants that happen to overhang the shore.

Manatees generally mate in shallow water. The period of gestation lasts between 150 to 180 days. Most often there is only a single calf, but sometimes there are two. Birth takes place underwater and may occur at any time of year. A newborn calf will be 2½ to 3 feet long and can weigh as much as 60 pounds. The mother immediately brings her offspring to the surface for its first breath; from then on, both parents care for the new addition to their family.

A young manatee sometimes rides on its mother's back. She nurses it for as long as eighteen months; nursing takes place underwater, and not — as scientists once believed — at the surface.

33

The body of a manatee contains meat that is delicious, leather suitable for a variety of manufactured goods, and oil of excellent quality. As a result, manatees have been heavily hunted in some localities and their numbers greatly reduced. The state of Florida now fines anyone $500 for killing a manatee. Unfortunately, this policy has not been followed in other areas. Adult manatees seem to have no natural enemies except man, but it is considered possible that sharks and crocodiles may attack the young.

In British Guiana manatees have been used to clear canals and other waterways of heavy accumulations of weeds and algae. In Georgetown, the capital, a few have been exhibited in the botanical gardens. They became quite tame and are said to have come a little way out of the water to take handfuls of grass from the tourists. It also is said that at night they made pathetic, groaning noises, much like the sound a cow makes when it wishes to be milked.

Dugongs differ from manatees in several respects. They are entirely marine, or sea, creatures and are never found in freshwater rivers. Their heads are proportionately larger than those of the manatees, their flippers shorter, and their tails sickle-shaped, rather than round.

There is only one living species of dugong: *Dugong dugon.* Its habitat is far removed from that of the manatee. It is found in the Red Sea, along Africa's east coast, around some of the islands in the Bay of Bengal, in parts of Indonesia, and along the northern coast of Australia.

Dugongs feed on marine algae and grasses which grow in shallow water. While feeding, a dugong rips out the entire plant, swishes it back and forth in the water until most of the sand is removed, then either swallows it with a little chewing or in a single gulp. Brown

African manatee
(*Trichechus senegalensis*)

seaweeds are usually rejected in favor of green varieties. Dugongs seem to feed methodically, rather than here and there in a haphazard way. Sometimes they pile whole plants of sea grass along the shore and, after they have accumulated a sufficient supply, return to eat them.

Most often dugongs appear in pairs or in small family groups of three to six. Their range is restricted by the sea grasses and algae on which they feed. They are easily frightened by noises, both those made above and below the surface of the water. Their sense of taste appears well developed, but like the manatees, their vision is poor. In color they are dark gray above and white below. They do not seem able to breathe through their mouths; knowing this, Australian aborigines catch them, plug up their nostrils, and asphyxiate them, instead of killing them with spears or clubs.

Like the manatees, dugongs are prized for their flesh and for the oil that can be extracted from their blubber. Many Eastern peoples believe that various parts of the dugong have magical and medicinal properties. On the island of Madagascar, for example, the inhabitants make a powder of the animal's upper teeth, then mix it with drugs and serve the mixture to people who have eaten contaminated food. In addition, they use fat from the dugong's head to cure headaches and take a portion of the blubber as a laxative. In parts of northwestern Australia people eat dugong meat whenever they get the chance; there, it is said, salted dugong and turtle eggs often take the place of our Western ham and eggs as a breakfast dish.

A full-grown dugong may weigh over 600 pounds and will reach a length of 8 to 10 feet. Its body yields from six to sixteen gallons of oil. In many areas dugongs have greatly decreased in numbers during recent years, and it is feared that continued hunting will lead to their extinction.

In that event, the last species of dugong will be gone from the earth. As in the case of another species, Steller's sea cow, there will be a few anatomical remains left in some of our museums for zoologists to study, and there will be a few descriptions and statistics that we can consult, if we are curious about what *Dugong dugon* was like.

George Steller left us the statistics of one giant sea cow he measured on Copper Island. It was 24 feet 7 inches from its nose to the end of its tail. The greatest circumference around its body was 20 feet 4 inches. Steller thought that a female sea cow of this size should weigh about 8,800 pounds. He probably was right, since he was a skilled and experienced observer. But, of course, if Steller made an error in judgment, we have no way of discovering it now.

Sea otter (*Enhydra lutris*) among floating kelp

# 5
# The Fate
# of the
# Sea Otter

Sea otter with baby

I N AT LEAST one vital respect, the sea otter (*Enhydra lutris*) differs from every other ocean-dwelling mammal. A layer of fat insulates the warm-blooded whales and seals against even the frigid waters of the Arctic and Antarctic oceans; the dugongs and manatees, though invariably found in tropical or subtropical seas, still possess a considerable amount of blubber beneath their hides. The sea otter alone lacks such insulation. It has only its fur coat to keep it buoyant and warm.

At least 2,000,000 years ago, when the sea otter first began to change from a land to a marine mammal, its fur coat, or pelage, may well have been thinner than it is today. As the animal adapted more fully to an aquatic life the number of hairs in its undercoat probably increased. Whatever the explanation, by recent times its fur had become more luxuriant than that of almost any other animal in the world.

For a long while the sea otter's thick coat was its good fortune. It enabled the agile, gregarious creature to multiply and to range for several thousand miles along the Pacific coast, all the way from Mexico and California in the south, to the Aleutian Islands and the Kamchatka Peninsula in the north and west. From time to time the sea otter was hunted by Indians and by Aleutian Eskimos, or Aleuts, who prized its meat and fur. But the Indians and Eskimos were neither greedy nor foolish; they had no wish to destroy such a useful supply of food and clothing through indiscriminate slaughter. For many generations these native hunters did no harm whatever to the huge herds of hardy animals living along what is now the coast of the continental United States, Canada, and Alaska.

In the middle of the eighteenth century, however, a change began to take place. By then the hazardous two-year voyage of the *St. Peter* was over, and the survivors were back on land. They spoke not only of the

37

strange, giant sea cows they had discovered in the Commander Islands but also of the herds of sea otters they had seen swimming in the waters of the northern Pacific Ocean.

It wasn't long before Russian fur traders, called *promyshlenniki*, appeared on the scene. They knew that in China, a country bordering their own, high prices long had been paid for a variety of animal skins. The emperor's royal costumes were made partly of furs; rich Chinese women wore fur capes; and mandarins and other important members of the ruling classes wore fur robes, belts, and sashes. The Chinese preferred sea otter to sable, fox, or marten, and they were able and willing to pay generously for their preference.

The Russian traders sailed from Siberia. They went to the nearby Commander Islands seeking sea otters. Then they went to the Aleutians and on to the coast of Alaska. The *promyshlenniki* did no hunting themselves. Instead, they hired parties of expert Aleuts to do the killing for them.

It took great courage and skill to hunt as the Aleuts did. Usually they went out in a two-man canoe, called a bidarka. This was a flimsy-looking, kayaklike boat, made of a wooden frame covered with walrus or seal skin.

The Eskimo hunters wore waterproof clothing made from the treated intestines of sea lions; to anyone watching a hunting party the need for such garments quickly became clear. First, the little boats left the shore and plunged straight through the breakers. As the bidarkas bobbed up and down, often among huge rocks just offshore, their occupants soon became drenched. Before the hunters could reach the calmer waters beyond the surf, their hats and jackets would be streaming with spray.

There were always several boats in a hunting party. The man in the rear of each boat did the paddling, while the man in front carried one of the metal-tipped spears used by the Aleuts.

The hunt was a cooperative venture. As soon as one of the marksmen had seen an otter, he hurled his weapon, often wounding the animal. Behind him, the oarsman signaled the other boats by raising his paddle in the recognized way. Immediately, the rest of the boats formed a circle, each boat a few yards from the first marksman.

The wounded otter invariably dived deep to elude the hunters. But sooner or later it had to return to the surface to breathe. From the nearest boat another spear was thrown, another paddle raised. A new circle was formed. Before long the struggle was over, and the dead animal was taken into one of the boats.

After the hunting party had returned to shore, the two oldest hunters examined the slain otter. The team whose spear was found closest to the animal's head was entitled to the prize, while the meat was shared equally by all the hunters. Soon the pelt would be in the hands of a Russian trader and would begin its long journey across the Pacific to Kamchatka or Canton and ultimately to the house of a powerful mandarin, or even to the palace of the emperor in Peking.

The Russian traders could not keep their activities a secret indefinitely. Within a few years word began to travel in many directions. One by one, Spanish, British, and American sea captains learned about the prize animal the Russians had discovered, and all of them made plans to capture as much as possible of the fabulous trade in sea otter furs.

During the last part of the eighteenth century the largely uninhabited territory of California was still a part of Spain's sprawling but feeble overseas empire. As more and more Russian ships appeared in Alaskan and Canadian waters, the Spanish authorities grew uneasy. They sent some of their own ships north to investigate. The sailors on one of them, the *Santiago*, brought along a supply of abalone shells. They traded these shiny objects to the coastal Indians for otter furs. After their return, the sailors sold the furs and found they had made a fortune. In this way the Spanish government discovered an enormously profitable fur trade on its very doorstep.

The Spaniards tried to keep the Russians, British, and Americans out of their territorial waters, but for the most part they had too few men and ships to succeed. However, the Spaniards still did quite well for themselves, despite the incursions of foreign traders. Spanish muskets managed to kill thousands of animals in California and northern Mexico. During a four-year period at the end of the century almost 10,000 sea otter pelts arrived in the Philippine capital of Manila for transshipment to China. These pelts enriched the Spanish government by more than $1,000,000.

A voyage of Captain James Cook had much to do with bringing the sea otter into greater prominence and with causing a quickening of the slaughter. In 1778 the famous explorer arrived at Vancouver Island while seeking the elusive Northwest Passage between the Atlantic and Pacific. Some of his crew traded with the Indians and obtained a quantity of sea otter skins. The Indians already had made many of the skins into robes, thus destroying their resale value. A number of other furs were used as bedclothes on the subsequent voyage across the

Pacific. By the time the ship had reached Kamchatka, two-thirds of the skins had been completely ruined. Yet so valuable was sea otter fur that those skins still in good condition brought the bonanza price of $10,000.

One of the ship's officers later wrote: "The rage with which our seamen were possessed to return to Cook's River, and by another cargo of skins to make their fortunes, at one time was not far short of mutiny."

A published account of this voyage encouraged other adventurers to visit the northwest coast of North America. The American Revolution was over, and Yankee ships already had begun to trade with distant China. At first, they rounded Cape Horn with New England cargoes, took aboard copper in Chile and sandalwood in Hawaii, and then sailed on directly to Canton. But the demand for furs, especially those of the sea otter, was so great that American ships began to make a detour. They stopped either in California or farther north in Oregon, Washington, Canada, or Alaska. By 1790 a sea otter skin — several feet of handsome black fur — was worth $80 to $120 on the Chinese market.

King Charles IV of Spain was not pleased with the news that American ships were operating in Spanish territories. He issued a decree forbidding trade in California and Mexico between Spaniards and foreigners. Spanish officials were forced to turn away American ships; publicly, at least, they had to refuse to deal with them. But the Americans did manage to trade on the sly and continued to obtain otter skins from the Spaniards. There were risks, though. One American captain was jailed for two years, and his entire cargo, including a number of fine otter furs, was confiscated.

American traders also were at a disadvantage because, unlike the *promyshlenniki*, they had no Aleuts to hunt for them. And so Yankee sea captains and their crews had to exercise imagination and ingenuity to gain a larger share of the spoils.

During the fall of 1803 a ship from Boston arrived in Kodiak, Alaska. The country was still a Russian possession. Captain O'Cain called on the governor, Alexander Baranov. He told Baranov that in Spanish California there remained an almost untapped hunting ground — sea otters by the tens of thousands. If Baranov would provide the Aleut hunters and their bidarkas, O'Cain would provide transportation. Later they would divide the profits.

Governor Baranov agreed. The captain took aboard forty hunters and twenty bidarkas and sailed south to San Diego and Baja California. By the summer of 1804 O'Cain was back in Alaska with 1,100 otter skins taken by Baranov's men; in addition, he had managed to purchase illegally 700 furs from Spanish officials and settlers.

The enterprise was such a success that other American ships soon joined in. One carried 150 Aleuts and seventy to eighty boats. Thousands of otters were killed in southern California alone. To the total were added many other pelts from more northerly sections of the coast.

The Spanish officials were outraged at these piratical activities and the loss of money they represented. But they could not halt the Russian-American scheme. Pelts continued to stream back to Alaska. The American ships even brought Aleut hunters into San Francisco's huge protected bay, where there was a large sea otter population. The Spanish fired on the hunters, killing and wounding several. But the hunting went on despite this interruption, and load after load of animals was carried off to the ships to be skinned and sold.

New schemes were tried and new expeditions sent to the Canadian and American coasts. The Russians established Fort Ross, sixty-five miles northwest of San Francisco, but the Indians nearby fired on the Aleuts for invading their hunting grounds. To the south there also was open warfare, with the Spaniards attacking or arresting the invaders.

Then Mexico gained her independence, and Spanish restrictions were lifted. The Mexicans had no wish to exclude foreigners; they only wished to share in the profits. So they granted hunting concessions in exchange for 50 percent of the "take."

Experienced American beaver trappers, however, found that they could avoid paying the 50 percent commission by temporarily becoming Mexican citizens. Having signed the necessary papers and sworn the necessary oaths, they slung their rifles across their backs and went hunting on foot along the shores of California, killing countless animals. Since these hunters did not use boats to retrieve the dead otters, many pelts were never recovered from the sea.

One year a large armed ship carried a party of law-breaking *contrabandistas* down from the north into Mexican waters. Without paying a commission, the Yankee freebooters fired muskets filled with buckshot at the swimming sea otters. Three hundred furs were taken in two months.

But a century of remorseless hunting had decimated the sea otter population, and the few survivors had grown wary of humankind. By the 1850's a white hunter complained that he "took only 32 sea otters from San Francisco to Monterey," where a few years earlier he would have been able to kill hundreds of animals.

As the sea otter neared extinction, Russian officials lost interest in Alaska. With this most valuable fur-bearing animal all but gone, and several other fur-bearers in short supply as well, why remain in such an inhospitable land, so many thousands of miles from the delights of Moscow and St. Petersburg? In 1867 William Seward, the United States Secretary of State, offered $7,200,000 for Alaska, and the czar agreed to the proposal. That year the United States purchased "Seward's Folly," primarily as a territorial buffer against possible Russian expansion. Although much criticized at the time, the purchase proved a great bargain because of the subsequent discovery of gold and other mineral wealth. By then the wanton destruction of one of Alaska's most enchanting natural treasures was already forgotten.

Despite its declining numbers, the sea otter continued to be taken by hunters for another forty years. By 1911 it was thought to be extinct in California. In distant Alaska the herds had grown so small that it no longer paid anyone to hunt them. Only then, with hardly a single animal to be seen along the entire Pacific Coast, did the United States, Russia, Japan, and Great Britain (on behalf of Canada) finally agree to end the killing. Not long afterward California passed a state law punishing with a fine of $1,000 and a year in jail anyone who possessed a new sea otter pelt. By that time, however, there were no new pelts for anyone in the state to own.

During the next quarter of a century no sea otters were sighted in California. Then, in the spring of 1938, Dr. Harold Heath received a telephone call at the Hopkins Marine Laboratory in Pacific Grove. The caller, Mr. Howard Sharpe, had just observed something puzzling. Looking down on a remote stretch of ocean beach near Carmel, he had seen some forty or fifty dark-colored animals swimming offshore. At first he'd thought they were the usual seals or sea lions. But after studying them through a small telescope, he began to have doubts. Their heads looked too flattened for seals. They had webbed hind feet and thick, bristly mustaches. They spent a good deal of time floating on their backs. A few appeared to sleep, shading their eyes with their paws, while the rest played. What kind of animals were they, Mr. Sharpe wondered.

So did Dr. Heath. Wasting no time on speculation, he snatched up a powerful pair of binoculars and drove quickly down the coast. And there they were, several hundred yards offshore — a herd of agile, frolicking animals — the first sea otters to be sighted in the state since almost the turn of the century. In all likelihood they were the descendants of a handful of animals that had escaped the hunters and remained hidden along some even more remote part of the coast; and now, having grown in numbers after several generations, they finally had reappeared.

Since 1938, the sea otter population in California has continued to increase. A census taken only a year ago estimated that there were just over 1,000 animals living offshore. Their range has grown too; it now extends for 140 miles along the coast.

The sea otter also has made a partial comeback in the northern Pacific. Some 30,000 animals now are believed to be living in western Alaska and the Commander and Kurile islands. Currently protected by a worldwide hunting ban, they seem to be safe for the present, at least in their more remote habitats. Yet, after more than sixty years of total protection, their range in the northern Pacific Ocean is still only one-fifth its former size.

Observers agree that sea otters are sociable and intelligent animals. They spend most of their time in the water floating on their backs among large beds of kelp. They swim belly down only when they are in a hurry. Their webbed hind feet have flattened into broad flippers, and these are extremely useful when the animals are swimming or diving for food. But once ashore, neither their hind feet nor their forepaws are very serviceable. The animals appear awkward and clumsy on land, according to those who have observed them in Alaska. (At the time of this writing, they have not yet been seen ashore in California, where they remain extremely wary of man.) It is believed possible that the females come ashore to bear their young, but this is not known for certain.

Sea otters are active in the daytime. They live in herds of thirty, forty, or more, often just beyond the offshore breakers. At night they usually rest and sometimes wind strands of kelp around themselves to avoid drifting away in their sleep. They also doze from time to time during the day; when they do this, they place their forepaws over their eyes in a characteristic gesture that shades them from the sun.

Mature sea otters are about 5 feet long, including their tails. The males weigh between 60 and 80 pounds, compared to 35 to 60 pounds for the females. Their color varies from black to dark brown; often there is cream-colored fur around the head, throat, and parts of the chest.

For protection against the cold, sea otters depend entirely on the long, soft hairs of their undercoat and the layer of insulating air that becomes trapped among these hairs. If their fur grows soiled, sea otters lose both body heat and buoyance, and to prevent this from happening the animals preen themselves constantly.

Sea otters have large heads, short necks, and ears that are small and pointed. They are the only carnivorous animals with four incisor teeth in their lower jaws. Their molars are broad and flat and are well adapted to crush the shells of crabs, sea urchins, mussels, and snails — like the delicious abalone — which make up an important part of their diet.

It is hardly surprising that sea otters are accomplished divers, as are other members of the otter family. As a rule, sea otters dive between ten and sixty feet while hunting for the bottom-dwelling animals on which they feed. They may take four or five preliminary dives before locating a suitable prey. A deep dive can keep them underwater for thirty or forty seconds.

Sea otter dining on sea urchin Using a flat stone as an anvil, the sea otter breaks abalone shells on its chest.

Sea otters are one of the few animals to use a tool. Having found a large clam, for instance, a sea otter will carry it up to the surface, along with a small rock from the ocean floor. Then, while floating on its back, it will place the rock on its chest. It will use the rock as an anvil and hammer the clam against it until the shell breaks, exposing the soft, edible meat inside.

Sea otters are believed to begin breeding at about three years of age.

Courtship and mating take place in the water. As far as is known, gestation takes eight or nine months, and the single pup may arrive at any season of the year.

Compared to the young of most carnivores, a sea otter pup is born at an advanced stage of development. Its eyes are open at birth, and it already has a complete set of milk teeth. It weighs between three and five pounds when newly born. Although it nurses for about a year, it begins to take some soft food from its mother after just a few weeks.

A sea otter pup is carried, nursed, and groomed on its mother's chest, while she swims about on her back. She devotes great care to it, fondling it constantly and leaving it only to dive for food. Occasionally a pup becomes separated from its mother. When this happens, she becomes violently agitated and swims around screaming until they are reunited.

Though sea otters have been sighted again in California, the end of their story there may not be a happy one. Two dangers now threaten them. One comes from the oil and other pollutants that are making the ocean's water increasingly dirty. If the sea otters' narrow range becomes too befouled, the animals will be unable to groom themselves sufficiently to keep clean; they will lose buoyancy and warmth and eventually will die.

The other threat also is man-made. Because sea otters are such skillful hunters, they are able to find — and eat — a great many abalone. Few seafoods are more popular in California, and the number of abalone brought to market has been declining ever since the sea otter's return. Abalone divers say that the sea otters are depriving them of their livelihood. Along with a certain number of seafood-lovers, they insist that the sea otters either must be killed or captured and taken to another part of the coast.

Fortunately the sea otters have a growing army of friends. A special organization has been formed with the sole purpose of helping their cause. And various individuals and environmental groups also are working to see that current laws protecting the sea otter are not changed.

What the outcome of these legal struggles will be no one can say. Should they be lost, or should the offshore waters become too polluted, the sea otters will finally be gone from California. Then, in order to see any of these rare and engaging sea mammals a person will have to travel several thousand miles across the Pacific to western Alaska and the islands beyond.

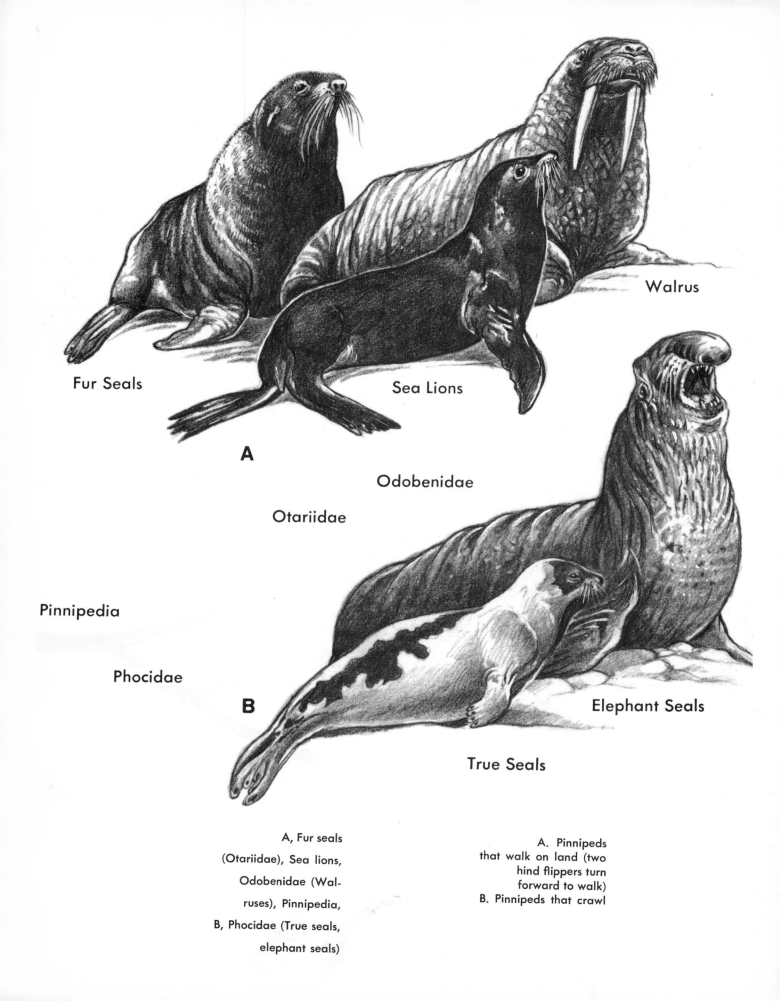

Fur Seals

Sea Lions

Walrus

**A**

Odobenidae

Otariidae

Pinnipedia

Phocidae

**B**

Elephant Seals

True Seals

A, Fur seals
(Otariidae), Sea lions,
Odobenidae (Wal-
ruses), Pinnipedia,
B, Phocidae (True seals,
elephant seals)

A. Pinnipeds
that walk on land (two
hind flippers turn
forward to walk)
B. Pinnipeds that crawl

# 6
# And One for the Circus

Seal balancing ball

ABOUT 30,000,000 years ago the first seallike animals began to dwell in the oceans of the world. Since then their descendants have changed and multiplied. Today they form the order of sea mammals called Pinnipedia — a word meaning fin-footed. Among various members of the order are the sea lions, the fur seals, the walrus, the elephant seals, and a number of so-called "true" seals. At first glance it is a large and confusing group of animals.

Actually, though, there are just two main kinds of pinnipeds — those that walk on land, and those that crawl. The "walkers" include several species of sea lions, the different fur seals, and the walrus. The "crawlers" include the huge elephant seals and the true seals in all of their great variety.

There is one basic anatomical difference between pinnipeds that walk and pinnipeds that crawl. A walker has two hind flippers which can be turned forward to be used on land along with the animal's fore flippers. But a crawler cannot turn its hind flippers forward. On land it must drag itself ahead, sometimes at a much slower pace, through the use of its fore flippers alone.

Among the walking pinnipeds there are two separate families. One family, the Otariidae, consists of the sea lions and the fur seals. The second family, the Odobenidae, consists solely of the walrus.

Sea lions and fur seals have several common physical characteristics, so that it is not always easy to tell them apart. All sea lion and fur seal

47

species have small external ears. They have streamlined, torpedo-shaped bodies that are well adapted to a marine life. Their claws are small, and they have thick, cartilaginous flippers that measure more than one-fourth the length of their bodies. Like their cousin the walrus, all sea lions and fur seals can walk or run in a sort of doglike position.

But in one significant way sea lions and fur seals differ greatly from one another. The fur seal, as its name implies, has a thick, warm underfur of great commercial value. In contrast, the sea lion has hardly any underfur, so that its pelt can be utilized for little except leather. Despite this, certain kinds of sea lions have not escaped exploitation. Like several other marine mammals, they have been hunted extensively at one time and another for the valuable oil contained in their blubber.

Different species of sea lions live in the Northern and Southern hemispheres. By far the most numerous species below the equator is *Otaria byronia*, the southern sea lion. This animal has a range of more than 6,000 miles. It is found from Brazil, on the eastern coast of South America, south to Cape Horn, and then north again, along the continent's west coast, as far as Peru.

There are thought to be from 750,000 to 1,000,000 southern sea lions at the present time. Their abundance is probably the result of two factors: Their fur is of little value, and when ashore they live in rocky and inaccessible places, where hunters find it difficult to land.

Most sea lions remain near salt water, but occasionally an animal will travel in fresh water for a considerable distance. One southern sea lion was seen swimming in the Río de la Plata at a spot more than 150 miles from the ocean.

**Pod of young sea lions**

Sea lions use their fore flippers as oars or paddles. At slow speeds they bring only these flippers into play. To go faster the animals use their hind flippers too.

In many pinnipeds the male is considerably larger and heavier than the female, and this is true of the southern sea lion. An adult male weighs between 600 and 700 pounds; an adult female weighs but 300. The male grows to a length of 8 feet, the female to a length of 6. In coloring the two sexes also differ. Males usually are dark brown, with a mane of lighter color and a belly of dark yellow or gold. Females are dark brown, with yellow coloring about the neck and head.

Sea lions live the year around in herds and are seldom found alone. During the nonbreeding season a herd of southern sea lions remains unorganized. But as the Antarctic summer draws near, animals of breeding age begin to separate from those that are too old or immature — a form of behavior that is characteristic of other sea lion species and of the fur seals too.

Before long all suitable parts of the rocky coastline are filled with rookeries, or breeding areas. Inside each rookery a number of harems are formed. Each of these consists of a large breeding bull and several mature cows.

49

Shortly after the cows come ashore and enter a harem they give birth to their pups. Then the cows mate with the breeding bulls. Observers report that among southern sea lions there is an average of nine cows per harem.

During the breeding season each harem bull guards his females against the mating attempts of other bulls. This leads to numerous fights, many of them extremely bloody. A harem bull will not leave his territory, even when a rising tide threatens to cover his entire body. By the time the breeding season is over he has been without food, and almost without sleep, for two months. He is much thinner, for he has been living solely off the huge rolls of blubber around his throat and chest.

Southern sea lion pups are about 2½ feet long at birth. Females usually have only one pup each year; twins are rare. Most pups are born within a three-week period from Christmas Day to the following January 15.

After the harems break up in February, the females return to the sea to find nourishment; from time to time they land again and suckle their young. While their mothers are at sea, the pups wander around the rookery, collecting in groups, or "pods." They divide their time between sleeping and playing. They do not enter the water until

**Australian sea lion (Neophoca cinerea)**

coaxed by their mothers, and even then, when they find themselves in deep water, they try to escape by climbing onto their mothers' backs.

The death rate for the young is high among sea lions and fur seals. Within the first few weeks a number of pups die of starvation. This almost invariably happens if a pup loses its mother, for no other female will feed the orphan unless she already has lost her own offspring. Pups also die from different kinds of parasitic worms and from being crushed by the heavy bulls in the rookeries.

The southern sea lion feeds a great deal on squid. Small fish and crustaceans are eaten too, as well as an occasional penguin. The animal has a peculiar habit that may be associated with eating. In common with other pinnipeds, the southern sea lion is a "stone-swallower." During its lifetime it will swallow as much as twenty pounds of assorted stones and pebbles.

No one is certain why pinnipeds do this. According to one theory, when the animals are thin and weigh less than normal, they swallow stones for ballast. An alternate theory suggests that only a fat and excessively buoyant animal swallows stones. Supposedly, the weight of the stones then helps the animal swim more easily underwater. But there is no proof of either theory, and the mystery of stone-swallowing remains unsolved.

Two other sea lion species live in the Southern Hemisphere. Neither is numerous or well known. The Australian sea lion (*Neophoca cinerea*) has a range extending westward from the city of Adelaide along the southern coast of Australia. The other, Hooker's sea lion (*Phocarctos hookeri*), lives only around New Zealand and the neighboring islands to the south.

The Australian sea lion is a large animal, the more graceful female reaching a length of 10 feet, the more powerful male a length of 12. Their mating season lasts from October to December, and there are four or five females to a harem. The breeding bulls of this species do not fast during the breeding season but continue to catch and eat penguins, along with fish, the main item of their diet. Like other pinnipeds, these sea lions are stone swallowers — small stones found in their stomachs have been the size of walnuts; bigger stones, usually taken from older animals, have been the size of tennis balls.

Hooker's sea lion is a smaller animal. The male may grow to 10 feet, the female to 6. Flounders, other kinds of bottom fish, mussels, and crabs are said to be their principal food.

51

Hooker's sea lion (*Phocarctos hookeri*)

Observers have noticed that Hooker's sea lion has two odd and not particularly endearing feeding habits. While at sea the animal sometimes dines on a local species of red crab, *Nectocarcinus antarcticus*. Then it returns to shore and regurgitates a ball of indigestible crab legs and claws. The animal also has been seen catching numbers of penguins along the beach. After a successful chase, it tears the bird to pieces, discards unwanted bones and skin, and swims out to sea to enjoy a leisurely meal.

Today Hooker's sea lion is rarely seen. A recent publication of the British Museum, *Seals of the World*, accounts for the species' current scarcity in this way: "During the 19th century, when sealing activities in the southern hemisphere were at their height, Hooker's sea lions were included in the general slaughter, oil being obtained from their blubber, and the skins used for leather." At the present time, 10,000 of these animals may be all that are left in the world.

Two species of sea lions live in the Northern Hemisphere, and one is very familiar to us. It is the Californian sea lion (*Zalophus californianus*), the playful "trained seal" that we see in zoos and circuses. With few exceptions, it is the only pinniped that has been trained to perform.

Until recently, Californian sea lions could be found in three widely separated parts of the world. A tiny population of 300 inhabited the waters of Japan around the island of Honshu. Some experts believe this branch of the family is now extinct. Another colony of about 20,000 animals still lives in the Galápagos Islands, west of the coast of Ecuador. And the largest number, perhaps 50,000 animals, lives in California.

The Californian sea lion, an exclusively coastal animal, is hardly ever found farther than ten miles from land. During the winter many of the bulls move north for a time. They have been sighted in Oregon and Washington and near Vancouver, British Columbia.

An adult female weighs 200 pounds; an adult male weighs 600. He is about a foot longer, reaching maximum length of 7 feet. Man is the leading enemy of these sea lions, although sharks and killer whales (*Orcinus orca*) also take a number of victims.

Animals in the wild experience a variety of sicknesses, and Californian sea lions are no exceptions. Among other conditions, they suffer from heart disease and from severe gastric ulcers. Some authorities suggest that these ulcers may be caused by the sharp stones the animals swallow. Whatever the original cause, the ulcers are kept in a state of chronic irritation by the numerous parasites that live in the animals' stomachs. In captivity, the ulcers can be treated effectively by modern medical techniques.

Generally, Californian sea lions feed on squid and octopus. They also are agile enough to catch herring, rockfish, hake, and an ugly creature called a rat fish. It now is thought possible that their whiskers act as a kind of sonar, telling them which prey is suitable and which is not. They do not bellow or roar, as other sea lions do, but "speak" in a barking voice.

Few animals are more pleasing to watch than Californian sea lions. They are extremely playful and often chase and catch their own air bubbles in the water. They are intelligent and have good memories. It may take a year to train an animal to perform, but even after a layoff of several months, it will still remember the tricks it has learned. Californian sea lions have lived more than twenty years in captivity. Their performing life is said to be between eight and twelve years, and dur-

A colony of California sea lions (*Zalophus californianus*)

Californian seals near feeding time at the zoo

ing that time their antics in zoos and circuses give pleasure to millions of people.

Northern — Steller's — sea lion (*Eumetopias jubatus*) is the other species that lives above the equator. It is probably the heaviest of all sea lions, a mature male weighing as much as a ton. These sea lions are belligerent and are not considered suitable for circus training. They have scarcely any enemies except man; even killer whales are reluctant to attack any but lone or immature animals.

The northern sea lion resembles its counterpart, the southern sea lion, in many ways. It too has a vast range — from Japan, in the western Pacific, through the Aleutian chain, then along the coasts of Canada and the United States, as far as southern California. Large-size breeding colonies now are found in the Pribilof Islands and in the nearby Aleutians, where there may be as many as 100,000.

Complaints have been made by commercial fishermen that Steller's sea lions feed heavily on salmon, and for this reason many of the animals have been killed. A number of recent studies, though, indicate that most of these complaints have been exaggerated. The animals do feed sporadically on salmon; they also feed on herring, halibut, flounder, sculpin, pollack, cod, and lampreys — the last a large, voracious, parasitic eel, which causes a considerable number of deaths in the salmon population. For that reason alone, exterminating entire herds of sea lions has probably not helped the complaining fishermen.

Despite the fact that it was far from the most valuable marine mammal, Steller's sea lion was killed in great numbers during the

55

Southern sea lion
(*Otaria byronia*)

nineteenth century. One American who hunted the animal was Captain Charles Scammon. Later he wrote a unique account of his experiences in the Pacific.

> None but the adult males [he wrote] were captured, which was usually done by shooting them in the ear or near it; for a ball in any other part of the body had no more effect than it would on a grizzly bear. . . . A few years ago, great numbers of sea lions were taken along the coast of Upper and Lower California, and thousands of barrels of oil obtained. The number of sea lions slain exclusively for their oil would appear fabulous, when we realize the fact that it requires . . . the blubber of three or four sea lions to produce a barrel of oil. . . .

Obviously, when these sea lions were killed, little was saved except the blubber. Except possibly for the skins, the remainder was considered waste and was left for the sea gulls and other scavengers.

Far to the north, the natives of Alaska put the sea lions to better use. Captain Scammon had been there too. He wrote of the Aleuts and their methods:

56

The dead animals are skinned, and their hides packed in tiers, until . . . they are stretched on frames to dry, and eventually become the covering or planking for the Aleutian *baidarkas*. . . . The fat is taken off and used for fuel, or the oil is rendered to burn in their lamps. The flesh is cut into thin pieces from the carcass, laid in the open air to dry, and becomes a choice article of food. The sinews are extracted, and afterward twisted into thread. The lining of the animal's throat is put through a course of tanning, and then made into boots, the soles of which are the under covering of the sea lion's fin-like feet. The intestines are carefully taken out, cleaned, blown up, stretched to dry, then tanned, and worked into water-proof clothing. The stomach is emptied of its contents, turned inside out, then inflated and dried for oil-bottles, or it is used as a receptacle for the preserved meat; and what remains of the once formidable animal is only a mutilated skeleton.

And yet — "mutilated" or not — how complete was the utilization of the sea lion's body. Living in a harsh world, with little margin for waste, the Aleuts discovered every conceivable use for the animal, overlooking nothing that was salvageable. Perhaps for those millions of us who must live today in a world of growing populations and diminishing resources, the techniques of the "primitive" Aleutian people might be worth at least a moment's passing consideration.

Caspian seal
(*Pusa caspica*)

57

Alaskan, or northern,
fur seal (*Callorhinus
ursinus*)

# 7
# Fur Seals,
# North and South

A fur seal pup

THE FUR SEALS of the world can be conveniently divided into two separate but related animal subfamilies. One of these, consisting of seven species, lives almost exclusively in the Southern Hemisphere. Its members are found along the coasts of Africa, South America, Australia, and on a number of remote islands near Antarctica. The other subfamily inhabits the Northern Hemisphere. It consists of only a single species, which lives in a vast region of the Pacific Ocean. This animal, *Callorhinus ursinus*, is variously called the Alaska, the northern, or the Pribilof fur seal. It is more numerous than its southern relatives, and its fur is more luxurious than any of theirs.

Few large wild animals, and certainly no other pinniped, has been studied as thoroughly as the Alaska fur seal. Its migrations have been mapped, its breeding colonies observed, its bodily parts subjected to literally thousands of tests and examinations. It has been "farmed" for several decades by the United States Department of the Interior under international treaty, and while fierce controversy currently surrounds this activity, many well-informed authorities point to it as a rare example of enlightened wildlife conservation.

The Alaska fur seal is a handsome animal. Males grow to a length of 7 feet, females to 5. Mature males are much heavier, weighing 600 pounds to a mere 130 for the females. In color the two sexes also differ considerably. Adult males are a rich, deep brown, while females have dark-gray backs and chests of light gray mingled with light brown.

There are three breeding places where the animals gather each year: the Pribilof Islands, north of the Aleutians, in the eastern Bering Sea; the Commander Islands, in the western Bering Sea; and Robben Island, between Japan and Siberia, in the Sea of Okhotsk.

During their annual feeding migration, most of the fur seals from the Commander Islands and Robben Island move down the Japanese coast, while most of the Pribilof herds move along the eastern coast of

the Pacific Ocean. But the three groups do not remain completely separate. Individuals pass from one group to another, so that unless they have previously been tagged, it is not always clear which animals "belong" to the interested parties — to Russia, Canada, or the United States. In all likelihood this uncertainty has encouraged international cooperation. The herds now are managed with treaty restrictions in mind, including those animals that breed on United States territory, in the Pribilof Islands.

The annual migration of Alaska fur seals from the Pribilofs begins in October. Some mature females leave by then, but most of the animals remain until November. A month later, the last of the herds have disappeared from the islands of St. George and St. Paul.

The Alaska fur seal travels alone or in small herds of ten or less. For a short distance the animals can swim at least ten or fifteen miles an hour, but their top speed is not known. Adult bulls make the shortest journey. They leave the Bering Sea through Unimak Pass, enter the Pacific Ocean, and swim eastward to the nearby Shumagin Islands to spend the winter and spring.

There are comparatively few of these adult bulls. The ones that swim to the Shumagins have survived the first year of life, when many pups of both sexes die a natural death. They also have survived the years when they might have been among the "bachelors" killed on the Pribilofs in the annual drive to thin out the herds. Only three or four of every hundred males survive these hazards to reach the age of ten, the average for a harem bull.

Food is abundant in the waters around the Shumagin Islands, and here the bulls rapidly regain the weight they have lost during the previous breeding season. No females or immature males are to be seen, though, because these smaller fur seals, lacking sufficient blubber, cannot endure the cold northern weather, as the big bulls can.

The females and the young continue south on their individual journeys, some animals traveling as far as the vicinity of San Francisco. During the migration they take many different foods, most often herring, squid, pollack, and lantern fish. Mature Alaska fur seals are powerful divers; they have been discovered at depths of up to 240 feet. Experts are not certain, but they believe that the migrating animals feed mostly at night and sleep during the day.

In April the dispersed animals begin to travel north again, and by May large numbers have returned through Unimak Pass to the Bering Sea. There are fewer of them, however, than left in the fall, for numerous individuals have been eaten by killer whales and by white sharks (*Carcharodon carcharias*). By the time they return, some animals will have traveled 6,000 miles, a longer migration than that of any other pinnipeds.

Around the beginning of June the bulls clamber noisily ashore again in the Pribilofs. Many of these animals return to the same rookeries year after year. They roar, fight, establish their territories, and toward the middle of the month, when the mature females arrive, the rookeries have been organized. By then the harem bulls have their stations staked out, and the bachelors — those not quite strong enough to match the aggressiveness of their elders — loiter around the fringes, ready to take over any stray females that are allowed to wander off.

Two or three days after returning to the islands a cow gives birth to a single pup. Delivery time is about ten minutes, and the pup usually is born head first. The mother is attentive for several days. She smells her pup carefully in order to be able to identify it later, and she pulls it out of danger when other animals come too close. The bulls are totally indifferent to the young, and the mothers, after about a week, lose most of their interest too, except when they feed their offspring. For about two months the harem bulls bellow, threaten, fight, and mate with as many as fifty cows, never once leaving their stations to feed.

The pups are about 2 feet long at birth and weigh an average of 12 pounds. The peak of the pupping season comes between June 20 and July 20. At first the pups have coarse black hair, but after eight weeks moulting takes place. The next coat is steel gray, with creamy white hairs on the chest. By then a pup's coat has become a complicated structure that only fur seals possess; it now contains bundles of fur fibers, each bundle protected by a stiff guard hair. The handsome, shiny coat that is visible is really composed of these guard hairs, and not of the soft, valuable fur that lies hidden underneath.

Five hundred thousand fur seal pups are born annually in the Pribilofs, but the death rate is high. By the end of the first year as many as half may have died; as many as 70 percent may be dead before the end of the third year. Hookworm infestation causes the most deaths among the pups in the rookeries. Dysentery kills many more. A few young animals are trampled to death, and an estimated 1 percent die of starvation. Mortality rates vary greatly from year to year. Biologists have counted as few as 17,000 dead pups in the rookeries and as many as 120,000.

At the same time that the pups are being born, the commercial sealing season begins. This controversial activity lasts from four to five weeks and is supervised by government observers. During the sealing drives, only bachelor fur seals are killed, and they must be animals between 41 and 45 inches in length. Approximately two-thirds of these bachelors are three years old, about a third are four years old, and a few are either two or five years old. These animals have the best-quality furs and skins unmarked with battle scars. Because of the fur seals' polygamous habits, killing the excess bachelors in no way diminishes the health of the herds. It also prevents overpopulation, which would lead to an increase in starvation. Overall, 60,000 bachelors are killed annually, and at different times 30,000 excess females are also killed. The money realized by sealing helps the Pribilof natives to make ends meet and also is used to pay supervisory and research personnel.

The herds on St. George and St. Paul were discovered toward the end of the eighteenth century by the Russian explorer and fur trader Gerasim Pribilof. There were then an estimated 2,500,000 animals in the area. By the time the United States acquired the Pribilofs in 1867, unrestricted hunting had greatly reduced the herds. Subsequently, the Americans continued to slaughter the animals on land at an even greater rate; animals also were taken at sea, and this pelagic fishing was particularly wasteful, for there was no way to distinguish and protect the females.

By 1911 the herds had been reduced to about 130,000 animals. Since that year, with the exception of a period during and shortly following World War II, the herds have been protected by treaty convention. Pelagic fishing is now prohibited. To compensate Canadian and Japanese sealing interests, 15 percent of the Pribilof skins and an equal percentage from the Robben and Commander islands herds are sent to these countries annually. The current population on the Pribilofs alone is now estimated at 1,500,000 animals.

While more humane methods of killing could quite possibly be devised — and government scientists report that they are continuing to search for such methods — the charge of unlicensed cruelty raised by certain warmhearted but apparently poorly informed "animal lovers" hardly seems justified. The restoration of the Alaska fur seal is an almost unprecedented modern development. As a leading American biologist has said, it is "one of the finest examples of conservation in action" — so fine an example, in fact, that it is almost unmatched.

Among the various southern fur seals, there is little or no seasonal migration. The only possible exception might be the case of the South American fur seal (*Arctocephalus australis*), which lives a part of each year on the tiny Antarctic island of South Georgia before departing for northern waters. All other southern species tend to remain the year around within a fairly limited range, returning to their favorite rocks and beaches after short feeding expeditions at sea.

The South American fur seal is a relatively small species; the adult males weigh but 300 pounds, the adult females scarcely 100. They are found from Brazil, on the east coast of the continent, to the Straits of Magellan, and then along the western coast as far north as Peru. Their range is almost identical to that of the southern sea lion. Each species

Kerguelen fur seal
(*Arctocephalus
tropicalis*)

keeps mostly to itself, but when there is a quarrel, the smaller but apparently more aggressive fur seal is said to be the winner.

By far the most numerous species below the equator is the South African fur seal (*Arctocephalus pusillus*). The present population may exceed 500,000 animals. African sealing began several hundred years ago, and at least twice the herds were so reduced that commercial activities stopped for lack of profits.

Government research began in 1946, and today the herds are better managed. The sealers are supervised, and much of the extreme waste and cruelty of earlier years is no longer tolerated.

The South African fur seal has a fairly high-quality fur. In the Southern Hemisphere only the Kerguelen fur seal (*Arctocephalus*

South American fur seal
(*Arctocephalus
australis*)

Australian fur seal (*Arctocephalus doriferus*)

*tropicalis*) has one of better quality. But the Kerguelen fur seal, which inhabits a few remote Antarctic islands, is protected now, and hunters rarely are allowed to obtain its fur. This formerly abundant animal was a victim of the nineteenth-century sealing slaughter; even under present protection, it is believed to number no more than 30,000 or 40,000.

Guadelupe fur seal (*Arctocephalus philippii*)

South African fur seal
(*Arctocephalus pusillus*)

Three additional species of fur seals live in the far reaches of the southern Pacific Ocean. Little is known about the Australian fur seal (*Arctocephalus doriferus*), which is found along the south coast of that subcontinent. The Tasmanian fur seal (*Arctocephalus tasmanicus*) is an even greater mystery. Until recently some experts said it was the same animal as either the Australian fur seal or the New Zealand fur seal (*Arctocephalus forsteri*). The latter, the third of these obscure species, is now, belatedly, protected by the government of New Zealand. A century or two ago the animal was killed in huge numbers. Today's population may have risen to 50,000.

The last and rarest of all southern fur seals no longer can be found in the Southern Hemisphere. In fact, for many years the elusive Guadalupe fur seal (*Arctocephalus philippii*) was thought to be extinct.

During the eighteenth century the animal lived in truly enormous herds on a number of offshore islands both above and below the equator along the American Pacific coast. It was hunted on Más Afuera and Juan Fernández, off the coast of Chile; in the Galápagos Islands on the equator; on Guadalupe Island, off Baja California; and on the Farallon Islands, off San Francisco. In the early 1800's, 7,000,000 ani-

Tasmanian fur seal
(*Arctocephalus
tasmanicus*)

mal skins — of fur seals and sea lions — were taken on the island of
Más Afuera alone. By 1880 the Guadalupe fur seal had disappeared.

In 1927 a small herd was sighted briefly around Guadalupe Island.
Almost at once it vanished. There were no further sightings for the
next twenty-seven years, and once again the experts' judgment was
that the species had become extinct.

The herd, grown somewhat larger, was rediscovered in 1954. A
curious fact probably accounts for the survival of the last remnants of
the species: On Guadalupe Island the fur seals spend their daylight
hours sleeping in caves and emerge only at night to feed. Apparently
this schedule has provided them with sufficient concealment. Today
the protected herd of Guadalupe fur seals numbers between 300 and
400. Perhaps, with continued good fortune, the number of these
nearly extinct animals will continue to increase.

Walrus protecting baby from polar bear (*Thalarctos maritimus*)

# 8
# "Old Ivory Tusks"

Baby walrus

NYONE WHO HAS READ Lewis Carroll's *Through the Looking Glass* knows what a walrus looks like. John Tenniel, the first artist to illustrate that classic, drew an animal wearing fashionable clothes of the Victorian age — a bow tie, a blazer, a waistcoat, and a pocket handkerchief — but he also added a pair of long tusks and a thick mustache to the portrait, trademarks which distinguish the walrus (*Odobenus rosmarus*) from other members of the pinniped order.

The walrus is a large sea mammal that now lives almost exclusively in the waters of the Arctic Ocean, close to the edge of the polar ice. Herds of animals — the males as long as 12 feet and weighing 3,000 pounds, the females 2 feet shorter and weighing up to 1,800 pounds — are found in Canada's Baffin and Hudson bays, in the Bering, Chukchi, East Siberian, and Laptev seas, and off the coasts of Iceland, Spitsbergen, Franz Josef Land, and Novaya Zemlya.

Walrus herds often consist of 100 animals or more. The bulls, cows, and calves migrate together. In the winter they move south, with the advance of the arctic ice pack; in the spring they move north again, as the ice pack retreats. While migrating, they often ride on the ice floes until carried too far off course; then the animals abandon the floes and swim off under their own power. During stormy weather these walking pinnipeds have been seen making their way laboriously across the snow. They have been known to travel at least twenty miles in this fashion before regaining the element they prefer.

The walrus has a thick, bulging body, a short neck, and a tough, wrinkled skin which grows to a thickness of 2½ inches. The animal's layer of insulating blubber can be 3 inches thick and may weigh as much as 90 pounds. The ivory tusks of the walrus — actually its upper canine teeth — grow to prodigious size: about 3¼ feet in length and almost 12 pounds in weight.

69

**Walrus (*Odobenus rosmarus*)**

When not in the water the walrus herd seeks shelter on islands, rocky coasts, and ice floes. The animals are excellent swimmers, and the adults can reach a speed of ten to twelve miles an hour. They make two kinds of sounds. One is a bellow that resembles the call of a St. Bernard. The other is a cry similar to the noise of a trumpeting elephant. They use their tusks in several ways: to haul themselves onto the ice; to defend themselves against killer whales in the water and against marauding polar bears (*Thalarctos maritimus*) on the ice, where the bears sometimes attempt to seize defenseless young walruses; and to dig up the food they need from the ocean floor.

Most often a walrus feeds in water no deeper than 250 feet. The animal's tusks probably are used to stir up the gravelly sea bottom, while its lips and the 400 hairs in its mustache are used to separate the food — especially various kinds of shellfish — from the mud and pebbles. Then the fleshy parts of the mussels and clams are sucked out and swallowed whole, rather than being chewed, while the shells are ejected from the animal's mouth.

On rare occasions the walrus also eats warm-blooded animals. The remains of young seals have been found in an adult's stomach, and the remains of young walruses have been found there too. But it is thought that in most cases these practices are indulged in only when food is extremely scarce. However, a very small number of habitual seal-eaters do exist. They are almost always male walruses, and because their skin and tusks become stained with grease they can be identified easily. The Eskimos sometimes kill these renegades to protect the local seal population.

Baby walruses are born in April and May. They are 4 feet long and weigh 100 pounds at birth. They nurse for a year and depend entirely on their mothers' milk during that time. After weaning, they may remain with their mothers for another year or two, because their tusks are still short and they cannot obtain sufficient food through their own efforts.

In former centuries the range of the walrus was much larger than it is today. The animal has been hunted for at least 1,000 years, and in some localities great numbers have been killed. Until recently there was a substantial population in the Gulf of St. Lawrence and on the Pribilof Islands. Before 1890, 12,000 pounds of ivory walrus tusks were taken each year in the Pribilofs alone; and during a five-year

Killer whale attacking walrus

period there, a fleet of American whaling ships, unable at times to reach and hunt their usual prey, killed 50,000 to 60,000 walruses instead. Today none of the animals are left in the Pribilofs.

There still is no international treaty to protect the walrus, although in Canada and Alaska the Eskimos are allowed to kill only a specified number of animals each year. But many conservationists feel that the number of kills permitted is too high. The animal's present population is thought to be between 45,000 and 90,000, with the number decreasing slowly and steadily.

The earliest walrus remains yet discovered were those of an animal that lived near Yorktown, Virginia, about 15,000,000 years ago. Clearly today's walrus is the descendant of an old family. Zoo keepers in Denmark and the United States, where walruses are sometimes kept, report favorably on the animal's disposition. A walrus, they say, is charming and friendly and is endowed with a strong sense of curiosity. One polar scientist has recently called the walrus "the most naturally affectionate of all marine mammals," adding that a young walrus in captivity "is not satisfied unless it can crawl all over you, even after he gets up to 1,500 pounds or more." A far different creature from the oyster-eating hypocrite of Lewis Carroll and John Tenniel — though perhaps in another few years it will be just as rare as its famous literary counterpart.

Walrus family

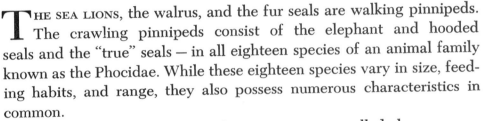

# 9
# Elephant
# and
# "True" Seals

Gray seal and baby

Tʜᴇ sᴇᴀ ʟɪᴏɴs, the walrus, and the fur seals are walking pinnipeds. The crawling pinnipeds consist of the elephant and hooded seals and the "true" seals — in all eighteen species of an animal family known as the Phocidae. While these eighteen species vary in size, feeding habits, and range, they also possess numerous characteristics in common.

The phocids, as these animals are sometimes called, have no external ears. They cannot turn their hind flippers forward, so that to travel across land or ice they must wriggle and hunch their bodies, propelling themselves as best they can by means of their fore flippers. This is such hard work that, if given the opportunity, many seals will roll or slide to their destination rather than crawl.

Most of the true, or earless, seals do not gather in large rookeries or form harems, as the sea lions and fur seals do. Unlike the polygamous walking pinnipeds, the adults of most seal species — although not the giant elephant seals — live in pairs, often mating for life.

The earless seals swim by means of their hind flippers. In short bursts they can reach a speed of twelve to fifteen miles an hour. They frequently swim on their backs and "stand" upright by treading water. Like other pinnipeds, the phocids can stay beneath the surface for considerable periods of time. To accomplish this an animal's circulatory system must undergo great changes. At the surface of the sea a seal might have a heartbeat of 150 per minute — twice the rate of a man. In a dive the animal's rate will fall to 10 heartbeats or less per minute, reducing the consumption of oxygen stored in the animal's

73

blood. This slow rate of oxygen usage enables the animal to remain underwater for an extended period of time.

Among the phocids there are some species that migrate and others that move only locally as they accommodate themselves to the changing seasons. The usual diet of the earless seals consists of fish, squid and other cephalopods, and various crustaceans. An animal may defend itself by opening its mouth, making threatening cries, and advancing on an enemy. Or it may choose to flee to the water's edge, where it can dive to safety. Family members tend to have good eyesight, a fairly sharp sense of smell, and — not surprisingly — rather poor hearing. Most earless seals lack the soft underfur of the fur seals, so that with the exception of two or three species, they are not hunted commercially. Seals are of great value, however, to the Eskimos, who prize them as a source of oil, clothing, and food.

Eight species of true seals live in the Northern Hemisphere. For the most part they are found in Arctic or Subarctic waters, where food is abundant and where their stiff coats and insulating blubber keep them warm.

The harbor seal (*Phoca vitulina*), also called the common, spotted, or hair seal, lives along both coasts of the Pacific and Atlantic oceans. In the western Atlantic it may wander as far south as New York City, and on rare occasions an individual has been seen off the Virginia capes and the Carolinas. In European waters it ranges from Iceland through the North Sea, the English Channel, and southward to Portugal.

*Phoca vitulina* spends most of its life close to shore. In more superstitious times it often was mistaken for a siren or a mermaid. And a harbor seal probably gave rise to the story of the Loch Ness monster, for single members of the species are known to swim many miles up inland waterways, such as the River Ness.

Fish is the main food of the harbor seal. In captivity the 6-foot animal has lived as long as eighteen years. Its life in the sea is probably shorter. Its enemies include Eskimos, killer whales, polar bears, sharks, and even sea eagles.

The gray, or Atlantic, seal (*Halichoerus grypus*) also is found on both sides of the Atlantic Ocean. One population center is in the Baltic Sea, the other around Newfoundland and in the Gulf of St. Lawrence. Single animals from Canada may wander far to the south, occasionally reaching Atlantic City, New Jersey.

Adult gray seals weigh more than 600 pounds and are 9 to 10 feet long. In common with most true seals, their color varies considerably.

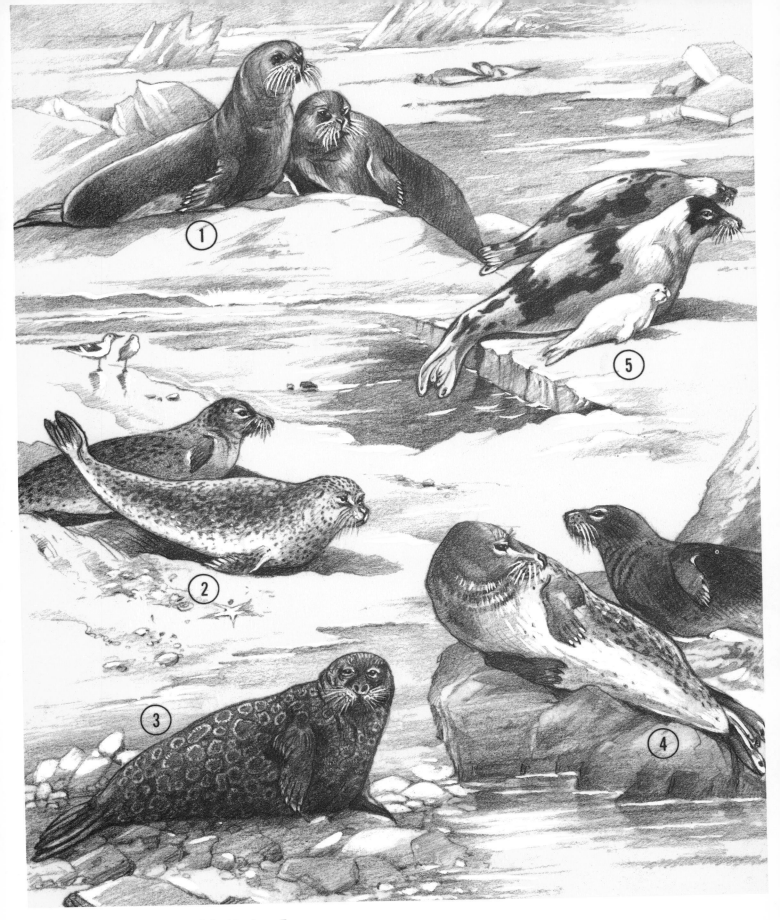

True seals of the Northern Zone
1. Bearded seal (*Erignathus barbatus*) 2. Harbor seal (*Phoca vitulina*) 3. Ringed seal
(*Pusa hispida*) 4. Gray seal (*Halichoerus grypus*) 5. Harp seal (*Pagophilus groenlandicus*)

They may be black, brown, gray, or silver, but because their coats can be used only for leather, the animals seldom are hunted.

Before they are weaned, gray seal pups, like the young of most pinnipeds, gain weight rapidly. Recently a female and her three-day-old pup were captured off the coast of Wales and kept in a pen on the beach. Each day measurements were taken. After two weeks the pup had gained 49 pounds. During the same peiod the nursing mother lost 95 pounds, an average loss of more than 6 pounds a day.

Now and again an orphaned gray seal pup is found on the beach. A few have been raised successfully. One was fed a daily diet consisting of one quart of cream, four tablespoons of cod liver oil, and one-half pound of margarine. Five times a day some of the oil and margarine were melted together, cream was added, and the mixture brought to blood temperature. Feeding was by bottle or tube. Quantities were doubled after the first week and tripled after the second. Small bits of herring were also added to the diet, and the pup thrived.

Leopard seal
(*Hydrurga leptonyx*)
attacked by killer
whale

Gray seals have been in the news very recently. Although their total population is only 30,000 to 40,000, in some places they have begun to overbreed. This has become true in the Farne Islands, off England's east coast. The animals there, after doubling from 3,500 to 7,000, are overcrowded and starving. Some 3,000 are considered excess; they soon will be killed, as humanely as possible. The action has been approved by Great Britain's National Trust and by other British organizations concerned with preserving wildlife.

Another northern pinniped in the recent news has been the Greenland, or harp, seal (*Pagophilus groenlandicus*). This animal is a notable diver, one specimen having been caught accidentally in a fishing net at a depth of 600 feet.

Harp seals occupy a vast range of ocean and coast, from Novaya Zemlya and Franz Josef Land in the Arctic Ocean, across the Atlantic to Greenland, and then south to Labrador, Newfoundland, and the Gulf of St. Lawrence. These migratory, 6-foot animals are extremely abundant. In the St. Lawrence area they are thought to number 3,200,000, with an additional 1,750,000 in the more easterly Arctic region.

It is the white-coated harp seal pups that have been much written about lately. Each year thousands of these defenseless animals, two to ten days old, are killed for their soft fur before moulting can take place. The manner of killing, as shown in photographs, is barbarous. It hardly makes matters more palatable to cite the economic needs of the local inhabitants or to speak of thinning the herds. Nor does it help to recall past figures: In 1831 a record 687,000 harp and hooded seals were slaughtered in Newfoundland alone.

Ten or twenty years ago the seal hunters were even more brutal than they are today. Formerly baby seals were kicked, gaffed, shot, and knifed to death. Today they must be killed by a blow, or blows, on the skull.

The baby harp seals, or "whitecoats," are helpless when the hunters come. They are still too young to swim, and so, unlike their mothers, they cannot leave the ice floes or the snowy shore for the safety of the water. A blow of the club, or perhaps several, and the 15-pound, 3-foot bundle of white fur is dead and ready to be stripped of its pelt.

Usually the mother seals do not attempt to defy the hunters. Recently, however, one mother did. Her pup already was dead, and when the hunter returned to strip it, dragging several other corpses behind him, he found the mother awaiting him — she had placed her own body over the body of her dead offspring.

The mother refused to leave. Two other hunters came up and stood a foot or so away. Still the mother would not abandon her pup. The hunters knew that legally no adult female may be harmed in a whelping area. So one of the hunters waved his club under her nose to distract her. As she lunged at the club, the others seized the dead pup and pulled it away. The mother followed, hauling herself awkwardly over the ice. But she couldn't go fast enough to catch up. Eventually she stopped, though she continued to watch them. Then she turned, dragged herself back to the water, and dived out of sight.

Today 180,000 harp seal pups and 80,000 adults are killed annually by Canadian, Russian, and Norwegian sealing vessels, and an additional 60,000 animals are killed on land. There is talk at present of reducing the take of the sealers, but what surely is needed even more urgently is a humane method of killing any excess animals. And the question must be asked: Is there any justification for killing the white-coated baby seals at all?

The remaining species of northern seals are relatively little known. One of them, a large animal that weighs up to 1,000 pounds, is the bearded seal (*Erignathus barbatus*). It is an unsociable creature noted primarily for its thick mustache, which gives it a slight resemblance to a walrus. Adults while underwater whistle to their pups. Why they do this and why they fail to do it on land are not yet understood. It is said that when they are about to dive they turn a preliminary somersault, but there is no explanation for this habit either.

Bearded seals have little commercial importance, but they are of considerable value to the Eskimos, who either eat the flesh themselves or feed it to their dogs. The intestines may be preserved and used as windowpanes. The hind flippers are boiled and eaten, and oil is extracted from the blubber and used in lamps. The liver, though, is discarded as poisonous, for it often contains so much vitamin A that a person eating a portion would become quite sick.

The ringed seal (*Pusa hispida*) lives in great numbers within the Arctic Circle. Less than 5 feet long and weighing but 200 pounds, it is among the smallest of the pinnipeds. Its color is gray, with black spots. A young ringed seal is born in March on landlocked ice, either in a den made in the snow by its mother or in a natural hollow in the ice. The mother seal makes a hole underneath the cavity so she can reach her pup without being seen by her enemies — men, walruses, polar bears, and arctic foxes. The Eskimos utilize ringed seals for food and clothing. They make harnesses, bags, and tents out of the animals' skins.

Two isolated pinnipeds are close cousins of the ringed seal. They are the Caspian seal (*Pusa caspica*), which lives only in the Caspian Sea, and the Baikal seal (*Pusa sibirica*), which lives in Russia's huge Lake Baikal, the deepest body of fresh water in the world.

Scarcely anything is known in the Western world about either species. There are perhaps 1,500,000 Caspian seals, and because local sealing is closely supervised, the animals apparently are thriving. The Russians have disclosed almost nothing about the Baikal seals, which are thought to number between 40,000 and 100,000 animals.

The last of the northern true seals is the oddly marked banded, or ribbon, seal (*Histriophoca fasciata*), which lives in the Bering Sea and in the Sea of Okhotsk. Like most earless seals, it is thought to eat squid, fish, and crustaceans. There are indications that the banded seal always has been a rare animal. Eskimos in Alaska kill a small number, using the meat for food, the skin for leather, the blubber for oil, and the rest of the carcass for glue and fertilizer.

One of the few pinnipeds to dwell in waters of the Temperate Zone is the monk seal. Within recent times there were three living species. The West Indian monk seal (*Monachus tropicalis*) was the first animal to be described by white men who came to explore the New World. Columbus, on his second voyage, found the 8-foot animals quite plentiful and killed a number for food. During the nineteenth century *Monachus tropicalis* was slaughtered for its blubber and skin. Since 1952 none have been sighted, and the species is believed to be extinct.

The other two species have nearly been exterminated too. The Mediterranean monk seal (*Monachus monachus*) is still seen in the Black, Adriatic, and Mediterranean seas, but it numbers only between 1,000 and 5,000 animals. The Hawaiian monk seal (*Monachus schauinslandi*) is even rarer. There may be no more than 1,000 or 1,500 animals left in the Leeward chain, to the northwest of the main Hawaiian Islands.

There are four species of southern, or Antarctic, seals, three quite numerous, and one quite rare. The Weddell seal (*Leptonychotes weddelli*) lives in large numbers — perhaps as many as 500,000 — on the Antarctic continent itself. The adult female is larger than her mate, weighing 900 pounds and reaching a length of 11 feet, compared to his 10. The young pups are comparatively large, being about 5 feet long at birth.

Killer whale after ribbon seal (*Histriophoca fasciata*)

True seals of the Temperate Zone
1. Hawaiian monk seal (*Monachus schauinslandi*) 2. Mediterranean monk seal
(*Monachus monachus*) 3. West Indian monk seal (*Monachus tropicalis*)

All winter Weddell seals can be heard calling to one another under the ice, where there are shelves on which they can rest and pockets of air which they can breathe. The animals are formidable divers. A Weddell seal has remained submerged for over forty-three minutes, and during a dive one individual reached the incredible depth of 1,800 feet. Dives of 1,200 feet are said to be commonplace.

The most abundant Antarctic seal is the crabeater (*Lobodon carcinophagus*). There are believed to be between 2,000,000 and 5,000,000, but no one is sure of their numbers.

Adult crabeater seals reach 9 feet in length. They are slim, light-colored animals which raise their young along the outer edge of the southern ice pack. Their name is not appropriate, for they feed on small, shrimplike animals called krill rather than on crabs.

Of all pinnipeds, the crabeater may be the fastest on land. Though one of the crawlers, it can move at an astonishing speed by beating the hard-packed surface with its hind flippers. Supposedly it can outrace a man for a short distance.

The leopard seal (*Hydrurga leptonyx*) is the least attractive-looking of the pinnipeds. A solitary animal, with a curiously reptilian appearance, it is the only seal to prey almost exclusively on warm-blooded creatures. Penguins are its main diet, but other birds and seals also are attacked and eaten.

Adélie penguins
(*Pygoscelis adeliae*), a
favorite food for the
leopard seal

Crabeater seal
(*Lobodon carcino-
phagus*)

Leopard seals usually feed in the water. Penguins are seized from beneath, shaken violently, and consumed. Apparently feathers and skins are devoured. There may be as many as 300,000 predatory leopard seals in Antarctic waters.

The fourth species of Antarctic seal is the very rare Ross seal (*Ommatophoca rossi*). This dark-gray animal, some 8 or 9 feet in length, is almost always found alone.

The Ross seal is a plump, pop-eyed species, which has been sighted on all sides of the Antarctic land mass. Why it makes its curious trilling and cooing noises is not understood. Indeed, very little *is* understood about this scarce animal.

The last of the phocids are the hooded, or crested seal and two species of a giant animal known as the elephant seal. The hooded seal, sometimes called the bladdernose seal, is a singular-looking creature of the Arctic and North Atlantic oceans. According to aerial surveys, some 300,000 to 500,000 are to be found between Newfoundland in the south and Greenland and the islands of Jan Mayen and Spitsbergen in the north.

The most unusual feature of the hooded seal is the grotesque nose bladder, or hood, of the adult male. When this enlargement of the nasal cavity is not inflated, it is slack and wrinkled and the tip hangs down in front of the mouth. When inflated, however, it forms a curious cushion, twice as large as a basketball, on top of the animal's head.

It is not clear why an animal blows up its hood. Anger, fright, or excitement do not seem to be the reason. In one case a 9-foot male was observed closely for two years. During that time the animal suffered a number of disturbing experiences. It first was caught in a net, then hauled aboard a ship, and finally taken to the zoo in Bremerhaven, Germany. There it was placed in an enclosure next to a roaring sea lion. Subsequently it attacked and tore the clothes off a zoo attendant, and one night it was badly frightened by the detonation of a nearby fireworks display. Yet not once during these events did the animal inflate its hood. In fact, it only did so at times of comparative serenity.

The largest of all the pinnipeds is the southern elephant seal (*Mirounga leonina*). Males are 18 to 20 feet long and may weigh more than 6,000 pounds. Females are 10 to 12 feet long and weigh approximately a ton. Forty percent of the animal's weight comes from a layer of blubber 6 inches thick. Like the hooded seal, the elephant seal has an inflatable nose hood. This may act as an echo chamber to increase the animal's roar. Certainly a large bull elephant seal can be heard several miles away.

Harems of up to 100 cows are formed on the Antarctic islands, where the southern elephant seals breed in September and October.

Hooded, or crested, seal (*Cystophora cristata*)

Southern elephant seal (*Mirounga leonina*)

The rookeries are extremely noisy, with harem bulls and younger bachelors hurling challenges and defiance across the bleak, rocky beaches. Fights are common, and many bulls are severely wounded. Among some closely watched northern elephant seals, however, all such wounds quickly healed, and there were no deaths among the combatants. In the northern herds that were observed most fights took place on land and lasted less than a minute. A very few fights, though, for top position in the herd lasted much longer. Sometimes a bull was bitten on the nose during a fight; and occasionally, while lunging at an adversary, an animal made the painful discovery that he had bitten his own nose by mistake.

At birth the southern elephant seal pups are 4 feet long and weigh 80 pounds. If the soil is not frozen, the pups make muddy wallows in which they spend a great deal of time, perhaps to ease the itching which accompanies the moulting of their woolly, black infant hair. Adult animals moult each year too, and during this time — thirty to forty days — they do not feed.

Sealing in the Antarctic began not long after 1775, the year when the island of South Georgia was discovered by Captain Cook. First the Antarctic fur seals were slaughtered there, and when they were almost gone, it became the southern elephant seals' turn. The latter were killed for their oil in such numbers that within a short time they too were reduced to near extinction.

After hunting became unprofitable, the elephant seal herds slowly increased again. By 1910 hunting was possible once more, but this time it was done under a licensing system. At present South Georgia is divided into four parts: Three parts are worked each year, and the fourth remains untouched. Cows and pups may not be killed, and a sufficient number of bulls must be left on every beach. The herds of southern elephant seals now number between 400,000 and 700,000.

The slightly smaller northern elephant seal (*Mirounga angustirostris*) has been less fortunate. Hunted even more ruthlessly than its southern relative, the species was reduced to a mere 100 animals by 1890. This remnant lived in a single herd on the tiny island of Guadalupe, 150 miles off the coast of Mexico's Baja California — the same island where the last herd of Guadalupe fur seals found a place of refuge.

For three decades the northern fur seal remained in concealment on the island. Since 1922 the Mexican government has given the animals complete protection, and because of this policy there has been an extraordinary population increase.

Today as many as 20,000 northern elephant seals live on both Guadalupe itself and on several islands to the north. Here the American government also extends full protection to the herds. Now these huge, ungainly pinnipeds with the curious nasal cavity seem to be reestablishing themselves successfully, and perhaps in the absence of hunters they may flourish again.

**Northern elephant seal**
*Mirounga angustirostris)*

# 10
# The Great Leviathan

APPROXIMATELY NINETY species of aquatic mammals belong to the animal order called Cetacea, the order of whales. They range in size from dolphins and porpoises to the giant sea mammals that were known collectively in earlier times as leviathan — the great whales which have been roaming the oceans of the world for millions of years.

The cetaceans, as they are sometimes called, can be divided for convenience into two large suborders: the Odontoceti, or toothed whales, and the Mysticeti, or baleen whales. Members of the Odontoceti — the huge sperm whale, and the innumerable dolphins and porpoises — all possess at least a few teeth in one or both of their jaws. With a single notable exception, they feed mainly on squid, octopus, and fish. The exception is the killer whale, whose diet consists of sea otters, seals, birds, and other whales, some much larger than itself.

By contrast, the baleen whales are entirely toothless. They possess, instead of teeth, a substance called baleen, or whalebone, a sort of modified mucous membrane which grows in a series of thin plates inside the whale's mouth. These plates act as sieves, or strainers. As a baleen whale begins to feed, it draws a large quantity of water into its mouth. The water contains countless small mollusks or crustaceans, often the cold-water shrimp, called krill. When the water is then ejected by the pistonlike action of the whale's tongue, the krill or other food remains entangled in the plates of baleen, ready to be drawn down into the animal's vast stomach.

Because cetaceans live entirely in the water and are well adapted to an aquatic life, they often have been classified as fish rather than

Moby Dick, a white Cachalot (see story of Mocha Dick, page 111)

87

Baleen, or toothless
whales (*Mysticeti*)
1. Gray whales
(*Eschrichtidae*)
2. Right whales
(*Balaenidae*)
3. Rorquals
(*Balaenopteridae*)

mammals. As recently as 1821, during the course of deciding a property case in New York City, a jury of twelve men declared that whales
were fish and not "animals."

But despite their somewhat fishlike appearance and their watery
habitat, both the toothed and baleen whales clearly belong among the
mammals. They are air-breathing animals, with lungs rather than
gills. They bear living young and nurse their offspring with milk from
their own bodies. They have a four-chambered heart and, with only
rare exceptions, have at least a few single hairs scattered about their
heads.

All cetaceans have torpedo-shaped bodies and front limbs that have
been modified into flippers. They lack sweat glands, have no external
ears and, unlike fish, do not have body scales. Their hind limbs have
long since disappeared. Their tail "flukes," or fins, are set horizontally
to their bodies, in contrast to the tail fins of fish, which are set per-
pendicularly. Cetaceans have a very thin outer skin and a thick layer of
oily blubber underneath, which helps them to maintain a constant
body temperature, even in the coldest polar seas.

Whales breathe through a "blowhole," which is usually located on
the highest part of the animal's head. Baleen whales have a double
blowhole, toothed whales a single one. When an animal is submerged

Toothed whales
(*Odontoceti*)
1. Narwhals
(*Monodontidae*)
2. Sperm whales
(*Physeteridae*)
3. Dolphins
(*Delphinidae*)
4. Beaked whales
(*Ziphiidae*)
5. River dolphins
(*Platanistidae*)

the blowhole is closed by a number of valves. Whales do not take water into their lungs and then blow it out, as people used to believe. The visible spout which is seen escaping from the blowhole is really only water vapor in the process of condensing as it enters the cold air.

Some whales dive to great depths and remain beneath the surface for long periods of time. To do so their bodies must undergo certain temporary changes. During a dive, the animal's heartbeat is reduced. A normal supply of blood apparently reaches the brain, but only a small supply goes to the other organs. The brain, in some unexplained way, remains unaffected by the accumulation of carbon dioxide in the rest of the body. Underwater the whale's eyes are protected against the irritating effects of salt water by a greasy substance secreted from the animal's tear ducts.

Whales have no sense of smell, and their vision is not particularly good, but their hearing and their sense of touch are of a high order. Recent studies have shown that at least some cetaceans are amazingly vocal — they produce many different underwater sounds: cries, calls, whistles, "songs" — and these sounds probably help the animals to locate food and avoid obstacles in their path. Because water is

Humpback whale with baby

an excellent sound conductor, some of these noises may travel great distances. Possibly they help males and females separated by hundreds of miles of ocean to locate one another during the mating season.

For various whales the period of gestation lasts eleven to sixteen months. Calves are born one at a time, and in most species they are from one-third to one-fourth the length of their mothers.

As soon as they are born, baby cetaceans must start breathing air. Probably most mothers help by pushing their newborn to the water's surface immediately after birth. At first, a mother swims on her side while nursing so that her calf can breathe. Later, baby cetaceans learn to nurse underwater. They grow rapidly, perhaps because of the high levels of fat, calcium, and phosphorus in their mothers' milk. Since they never leave the water, which supports the weight of their bodies, they eventually can grow to enormous size.

There are several giant animals among the baleen whales. One is the California gray whale (*Eschrichtius glaucus*), which reaches a length of 40 feet. Two separate populations are found. One spends the summers in the Sea of Okhotsk. During the winters it seeks out warmer waters, as most whales do, migrating south to the vicinity of

90

Korea. The other gray whale population feeds during the summers in the Bering Sea and then migrates some 6,000 miles to its breeding grounds in the lagoons and river mouths along the shores of northern Mexico and Baja California.

The gray whale is not a fast cetacean. On its migrations it normally swims about four or five miles an hour, but it can reach a speed of seven or eight when threatened. It is preyed on occasionally by killer whales. When these predators appear, the California gray whales may float belly up, apparently paralyzed with fright. Or they may head for shore and the safety of shallow water. They have become stranded in less than three feet of water without harm, being able to refloat themselves on the next tide.

California gray whale
(*Eschrichtius glaucus*)
on the ice

The gray whale has white streaks on its back and above and below its flippers. The outlines of four fingers can be seen in its flippers, which are large and rounded. The animal has large tail flukes and plates of baleen that are quite thick. Body lice infest its skin, and to rid itself of these unwanted guests the whale often rubs itself against a handy rock.

The California gray whale seems to be a playful animal. It enjoys rolling in the surf and sometimes hurls itself into the air, apparently out of sheer exuberance. An amiable disposition, however, did little to aid the animal during the early part of the nineteenth century, when it began to be hunted intensively for its oil and the sheets of whalebone in its jaws.

At first it was killed in the lagoons of Baja California by American Indians, who approached in dories to throw their spears. Later, white Americans used small sailboats and fired a gun that threw a lance and a bomb into the sides of the victims. Actually the California gray whale was hunted with a degree of ferocity that was unique even among nineteenth-century Yankee whalers. Knowing that a mother would not desert her calf, the American hunters deliberately singled out the calves in the lagoons and then slaughtered the mothers, too, as they tried to come to the rescue of their dying offspring.

By 1895, when the United States began to protect its gray whale population, the Baja California herds had almost been exterminated. The United States still protects the species, but across the Pacific it is hunted with little restraint by Japanese whalers. About ten years ago the California herds were counted as they passed San Diego on the way to their breeding grounds. Some 6,000 were thought to have gone by.

Among the earliest victims of the whaling industry were the bowhead, or Greenland, right whale (*Balaena mysticetus*) and its near relation, the Biscay, or black, right whale (*Eubalaena glacialis*). Both were clumsy, slow-swimming animals that could easily be overtaken, even by men rowing in small boats. After they were killed they remained afloat, unlike several other species of whales which sink immediately. This made it easy to "flense" them, or strip them of their blubber. And so they were called right whales, because, from the whaler's point of view, they were indeed the right whales to kill.

Today the Greenland right whale is rarely seen. A small population exists in northern Hudson Bay and another in the Bering Sea. Large numbers used to appear much farther south, particularly in the Atlantic Ocean off the coasts of Labrador and Newfoundland, but by 1900 these visits no longer were being made.

The Greenland right whale is a truly grotesque animal, whose mouth is 20 feet long, or about one-third the length of its entire body. It is a black whale that sports a cream-colored throat and chin. Usually it remains submerged for ten to thirty minutes, except when feeding. At such times it swims near the surface, where it engulfs great numbers of small fish or krill with a scooping motion of its jaws.

In earlier times an annual fleet of 200 to 300 whaling ships left various European ports to pursue the bowhead. A slain animal yielded seventy to eighty barrels of oil, at forty gallons a barrel—oil which was used ashore as an illuminant, in the manufacturing of soap and paint, and as a commercial lubricant. Some 1,500 to 1,700 pounds of baleen also were obtained from each animal for use in articles requiring strength and elasticity. When prices were at their highest a full-grown Greenland whale brought the hunters about $8,000.

The Biscay, or black, right whale, was hunted just as fiercely as the bowhead and is now equally rare. Though protected by the International Whaling Commission, it is believed to number less than 1,000 specimens.

Biscay, or black, right whale (*Eubalaena glacialis*)

The most singular feature of the Biscay whale is the odd-looking

Bowhead, or Greenland, right whale (*Balaena mysticetus*) being attacked by killer whales

"bonnet" it displays. This actually is an accumulation of numerous layers of hardened, or calloused, skin. In some animals the bonnet appears on the tip of the upper jaw. Usually it is infested with parasites, either small crustaceans or marine worms.

The last member of the right whale family is an extremely rare animal sighted only in the Southern Hemisphere near Australia and New Zealand. This is the pygmy right whale (*Caperea marginata*). About thirty-five specimens have been examined. The animal has thirty-four ribs, the most of any whale, and because of this and certain other anatomical features it is thought to spend an unusual amount of time underwater. Perhaps this habit, along with its relatively modest size, has enabled the pygmy right whale to escape the full interest of the whalers.

The most numerous of the baleen whales are now the rorquals, a family of giants which numbers among its members the largest animal that has ever lived on earth. The word "rorqual" comes from the Norwegian *ror hval*, meaning tube whale. The term refers to the grooves, or tubes, under the surface of the skin which run from the chin to the navel. No one is certain why rorquals have these grooves,

94

but they are all fast swimmers, capable of traveling at least ten or twelve miles an hour, and perhaps the grooves help to speed their passage through the water.

Some rorquals inhabit only the Southern Hemisphere, while other species inhabit both. During their annual migrations both northern and southern populations of the same species will approach the equator, but none are believed to intermingle. In the Northern Hemisphere the rorquals typically spend the summer near Norway, Iceland, and Greenland, then move down the coasts of Europe and America during the winter, traveling as far as Portugal, Virginia, and beyond. They mate and bear their young in tropical or subtropical waters and feed little, if at all, until they have returned to the polar regions in the early spring. Rorquals in the Southern Hemisphere spend their summers in the Antarctic, then travel north, toward warmer seas, as winter draws near.

One of the strangest-looking of the rorquals is the humpback whale (*Megaptera novaeangliae*). It has knobs on its jaw and head and around its huge flippers, which are about one-third as long as its body. The name "humpback" is derived from its short back fin, which takes on the appearance of a hump when the animal dives.

The black-and-white humpback grows to a length of 50 feet. It travels in schools, frequently within sight of shore. It is a playful animal

Pygmy right whale
(*Caperea marginata*)

which seems to enjoy rolling and sporting in the water. Now and then it lifts its flippers and slaps them down with a crash. Or it leaps from the sea and then returns to the water with a crack that can be heard miles away. In warmer seas particularly the humpback is plagued by vast armies of parasites, and like the gray whale, it seeks relief in rubbing its skin against projecting rocks.

The humpback was once of great importance to the whaling industry, but now it is almost extinct, numbering just a few thousand. Its voice has been studied by several scientists, and a commercial recording of its "songs" has been widely sold within the past year or two. Some scientists believe that these sounds are a form of language communication, perhaps of a sophisticated order.

The sei whale (*Balaenoptera borealis*) is an impressive animal, a fully mature specimen sometimes reaching a length of 60 feet. Its color is bluish black, and there are gray areas on the belly, throat, and sides. Baleen plates of the sei whale have an edge of very fine hairs which permit the animal to strain tiny fish out of the water. It is regularly hunted off the coasts of Korea and Japan, where it is known as the sardine whale, because of its prey. Never a particularly abundant animal, its numbers are believed to have been reduced recently by 50 percent, to 75,000.

The second largest of the rorquals is the fin whale (*Balaenoptera physalus*), a huge animal that can weigh more than 50 tons and measure more than 80 feet. It occasionally swims on its right side, a curious action which may account for an even more curious fact: While two-thirds of the fin whale's baleen plates are bluish gray, the other third,

Sei whale
(*Balaenoptera borealis*)

on the right side of the animal's mouth, are a creamy white. This sort of depigmentation occurs in fish and other aquatic animals, all of which have a tendency to be darker on their uppermost, exposed body portions and lighter on those portions hidden underneath.

Fin whales are gregarious and travel in large schools. Observers have seen hundreds of them in the same ocean area. Since World War II many fin whales have been killed by the whaling nations, Norway, Japan, and Russia; it is estimated that their numbers have shrunk during this period from 400,000 to 100,000, and the decline is being accelerated by the almost complete disappearance of the greatest of all the rorquals, the largest of the world's animals, the blue, or sulphurbottom, whale (*Sibbaldus musculus*).

This is a truly majestic animal. A full-grown cow, slightly larger than her mate, can reach 90 or 100 feet, almost one-third the length of a football field. Such an animal will weigh in the neighborhood of 125 tons, while its back rises 20 feet — three times as high as the tallest man.

Blue whales travel alone, in pairs, or in small schools of perhaps five

Blue, or sulphur-bottom, whale (*Sibbaldus musculus*) fighting giant squid
(*Architeuthis princeps*)

or six animals. Young adult specimens often travel by themselves. They are usually a paler shade of blue than older animals. Some people call the animal a sulphur-bottom whale because of the film of yellow-colored algae that grows on its underside.

Despite its massive bulk, the blue whale can swim at a speed of fifteen miles an hour. It lives almost exclusively on krill, and when it dines, it does so with a gusto appropriate to its size. After feeding, a 70-foot blue was judged to have 5,000,000 shrimp in its stomach, a dinner that weighed over 2 tons.

At one time the blue whale was the leading commercial baleen whale in the world. An average-size animal yielded seventy or eighty barrels of oil, and larger specimens naturally yielded even more. Fifty years ago blue whales were numerous in every ocean of the world. They were truly the monarchs of the sea, probably 100,000 of the most awesome animals the world has ever known.

Today there are thought to be between 100 and 1,000 in the world's oceans. Some experts believe that this is not enough for the species to survive.

Some species of dolphin
1. Risso's dolphin
(*Grampus griseus*)
2. Bridled dolphin
(*Stenella dubia*)
3. Porpoise
(*Phocaena phocaena*)
4. White-sided dolphin
(*Lagenorhynchus acutus*)
5. White-beaked dolphin
(*Lagenorhynchus albirostris*)
6. Commerson's dolphin
(*Cephalorhynchus commersonii*)

Common dolphins
(Delphinus delphis)
attitudes

# 11
# Whales
# with Teeth

THERE ARE SO MANY individual species of toothed whales that it is not possible to mention them all in a work of this length. The best that can be done is to describe the most important and curious of the dolphins, porpoises, and their near relations and to suggest some of their habits and where they can be found.

The words "dolphin" and "porpoise" are not always used with scientific precision. Generally, a sea mammal is called a dolphin if it is relatively small and has a beaklike snout and a slender, streamlined body. A porpoise is generally a small cetacean with a blunt snout and a rather stocky body.

Some river dolphins divide their time between brackish and salt water. The La Plata river dolphin (*Stenodelphis blainvillii*) lives along the coast of South America and in the estuary of the river after which it is named. The animal is about 5 feet long and weighs a bit over 100 pounds. In its long, slender jaws are two rows of fine teeth, between 210 and 240 in all, which are admirably designed for seizing and holding small fish.

A number of other river dolphins live the year around in fresh water. Comparatively little is known about such rare animals as the Chinese dolphin (*Lipotes vexillifer*), which is found only in a single lake in the Yangtze River, or the Amazon dolphin (*Inia geoffrensis*), two specimens of which were brought to the Fort Worth, Texas, zoo and kept there for a time in a covered pool. They appeared to be intelligent animals, alert and with good vision. Their calls to each other were quite audible to observers.

A large kind of porpoise, and one that is found only in salt water, is

101

Cuvier's beaked whale (*Ziphius cavirostris*). This is a medium-size cetacean, which reaches a length of 25 feet. It lives in all the oceans of the world and travels in schools of three to forty. Cephalopods are the principal item of its diet, and when it feeds, it does so on a considerable scale. One adult female's stomach was found to contain the remnants of 1,300 squids. Cuvier's beaked whale has never been hunted commercially, and it is mostly known from specimens that have become stranded because of accident or disease.

One of the largest of the porpoises is the giant bottle-nosed whale (*Berardius bairdi*), which may grow to 35 feet. It is a wary animal and difficult to capture. One harpooned specimen is said to have dived, at a terrific speed, to a depth of more than half a mile.

Common dolphin,

Common porpoise,

Bottle-nosed dolphin

Chinese dolphin (*Lipotes vexillifer*)

Amazon River dolphin (*Inia geoffrensis*)

Bottle-nosed whale
(*Hyperoodon
ampullatus*)

Cuvier's beaked whale
(*Ziphius cavirostris*)

Beluga, or white, whale (*Delphinapterus leucas*)

The beluga, or white, whale (*Delphinapterus leucas*) is a curious-looking cetacean found only in the Arctic Ocean. Because it makes a low, trilling, birdlike call that can be heard very clearly above the surface of the water, sailors have long called it the sea canary.

As the beluga ages, the amount of melanin in its skin decreases constantly. In time this results in the animal's changing color, from black or dark gray to yellowish gray, and finally to white.

The beluga is a gregarious animal and travels in schools that may number in the hundreds. Gifted with a supple body, it can scull with its tail and swim backward. The beluga has considerable commercial value. Its blubber is used for oil, and its skin makes a high-quality leather suitable for boots and laces. The animal is a bottom feeder, where it finds such fish as flounder and halibut, as well as a variety of squid and crustaceans. In turn, it is preyed upon by killer whales.

Another and even stranger Arctic animal is the narwhal (*Monodon monoceros*). The adult male has a single spiral tusk that may reach 9 feet. No one knows what purpose, if any, this elongated tusk serves, but it hardly seems likely that the narwhal uses it to break holes in the

105

ice or to duel with other animals, as was formerly suggested. Probably the tusk is a body structure that simply has grown too large to have any useful function now.

One of the largest and most important families of toothed whales are the Delphinidae, a family that includes a number of the swiftest and most agile of all cetaceans. Some species are noted for their habit of leaping clear of the water. Others are distinguished by their speed, which in the case of the common dolphin (*Delphinus delphis*) has been timed at more than twenty miles an hour.

Among the Delphinidae, many dolphins and porpoises have a habit of following a ship at sea or of forming a frolicking escort ahead of it, perhaps because they enjoy rolling in the ship's bow wave. At times these animals gather in large schools that may number between 500 and 700. This is particularly true of pilot whales (*Globicephala melaena*), a species that seems to have an innate tendency to follow a leader. Often if one member of a school of pilot whales is struck by a whaler's harpoon, the wounded animal will rush forward, with the rest of the panic-stricken school following blindly in its wake. Should

Narwhal (*Monodon monoceros*)

this happen in shallow water, all of the animals are likely to become stranded. The pilot whale is now hunted commercially in Newfoundland, where some 3,000 to 4,000 animals, averaging 20 feet in length, are taken annually for their oil. During three centuries, from 1584 to 1883, about 120,000 pilot whales were killed in a single area around the Faeroe Islands, between Iceland and Scotland.

One of the best known of the Delphinidae is *Tursiops truncatus*, the bottle-nosed dolphin. This is the animal, commonly found along the Atlantic coast of North America, that has been kept for several decades in public aquariums and open-air "marineland" parks. During the past few years it has been the subject of considerable research. Scientists familiar with the bottle-nosed dolphin rate it an extremely intelligent animal which is quick to learn a great number of tricks and games.

Some experts believe that of all animals the bottle-nosed dolphin possesses mental capabilities that are closest to man's. The animal emits a variety of sounds in patterns that suggest it is "talking" to other dolphins. Some researchers even hope to learn eventually how to communicate with these friendly and obviously highly unusual animals.

The largest of the Delphinidae, and one of the most remarkable of all sea mammals, is the awesome killer whale (*Orcinus orca*). It is found in every ocean, though perhaps most frequently in Arctic and Antarctic waters. Adult bulls are said to reach a maximum length of 30 feet, but both males and females probably average closer to 20.

The killer whale has a large and distinctive dorsal fin, which can be clearly seen while the animal is cruising in search of prey. It hunts in packs of from three to perhaps fifty. Armed with ten to fourteen large teeth, it fears nothing that lives in the sea. Its mouth and throat are large enough to swallow a full-grown seal, a young walrus, or other small cetaceans.

When a pack of killer whales finds some seals or penguins resting near the water's edge, the whales first dive deeply and then surge to the surface, sometimes breaking ice three feet thick as they dislodge and hurl their unsuspecting victims into the icy seas.

Some of the slow-swimming baleen whales, though considerably larger and heavier, are quite helpless when attacked by these rapacious predators. Killer whales have been observed seizing a baleen whale's tongue, tearing it out, and then finishing their helpless victim off at their leisure. They are known to attack other whales behind the back fin, where they rip out huge pieces of flesh. On these occasions they may fail to kill their prey, but years later the victims still carry huge scars testifying to the attacks. Fish, cephalopods, aquatic birds, and sea otters are all included on the killer whale's extensive menu. Whenever possible, *Orcinus orca* eats about 5 percent of its body weight daily, and this can mean between 300 and 500 pounds of meat.

In the open ocean the killer whale is truly fearsome and powerful. One harpooned animal remained submerged for twenty-one minutes struggling against the line still sunk in its body. Another was found dead, entangled in a submarine cable, at a depth of almost 3,400 feet.

Yet within the past few years a different side of the killer whale's nature has begun to emerge. Several of them have been captured off the Pacific coast of North America and kept under scientific observation. They have become quite tame, recognizing their keepers and submitting to tests with a good-natured docility resembling that of their smaller relative the bottle-nosed dolphin. The tentative conclusion reached by some scientists is that many dolphins and porpoises feel no instinctive fear of people but rather are drawn by sympathy and curiosity in their direction. Considering how most cetaceans have been treated by mankind, it seems like a fatally trusting way for dolphins and porpoises to behave.

Killer whale (*Orcinus orca*)

RM WHALE -

Of all the toothed whales, none can compare in size or strength with the huge, strange-looking sperm whale (*Physeter catodon*), sometimes known as the pot whale or cachalot.

The Biblical animal that swallowed Jonah must have been a sperm whale, for none of the baleens has a gullet large enough to swallow a man. Full-grown male sperm whales measure up to 60 feet, females up to 30. The larger male weighs between 35 and 50 tons. Calves are usually born in temperate waters and at birth are about 15 feet long.

The sperm whale has from eighteen to sixty teeth in its lower jaw, and when the animal's mouth is closed these teeth fit snugly into sockets in the upper jaw. Sperm whales emit a variety of sounds, which

Sperm whale *(Physeter catodon)* after squids

109

have been variously described as "a muffled, smashing noise," "a series of sharp clicks," "a grating sort of groan, very low in pitch," and "a rusty hinge creaking."

Observers have seen the sperm whale lift its huge head out of the water to look and listen. A slow swimmer, it ordinarily travels at four or five miles an hour, but when hunted it has been timed at twelve. Mostly the animals live in groups, or harems, of fifteen to twenty, the harem consisting of a mature bull, some females, and a number of calves. On their migratory trips, though, between tropical and temperate waters, a school of several hundred animals may be formed.

Sperm whales feed mainly on squid and cuttlefish, with sharks, skates, barracuda, and albacore of less importance to their diet. Often they feed at depths of 1,000 feet or more. There they hunt the giant squid, and when the two animals meet, a titanic struggle ensues. Most frequently the squid is devoured, but many sperm whales carry on their skin the marks of such battles.

The beaks, or mouths, of squids are often found in a sperm whale's stomach. Occasionally a curious, waxy substance, called ambergris, forms around these beaks. Some experts believe this only happens when the beaks have caused a severe irritation in the whale's stomach; but other experts tend to think that ambergris can just as well be formed inside the stomach of a healthy sperm whale.

Ambergris is invaluable to the perfume industry, because it is a **Bottle-nosed dolphin** fixative that retains the fragrance of perfumes for a great length of **with baby** time. It is usually found floating in the sea, sometimes inside the de-

composing stomach of a dead whale. It is worth ten to fifty dollars a pound. The largest mass of ambergris ever found weighed just under half a ton, and the dream of finding a similar hoard apparently still persists among beachcombers.

Several other commercial products are obtained from the sperm whale. A substance called spermaceti is found in the animal's head, from which the finest quality candles and cosmetic ointments are manufactured. The head and blubber also produce about thirty barrels of highly prized sperm whale oil.

One of the most famous animals in all literature is Herman Melville's sperm whale, the symbolic giant Moby Dick. Melville, a former whaling man, drew on two sources for his nineteenth-century creation. One was the story of the legendary Mocha Dick, a freakish albino sperm whale long reported by sailors in the southern whaling fisheries. The other was the tragic tale of the whaling ship *Essex*, out of Nantucket, that arrived in the Pacific Ocean in 1821. There it found a harem of sperm whales, several of which were harpooned. The captain and second mate of the *Essex* were in two of the ship's boats busily securing their prizes, when a huge, unwounded male appeared. Probably it was the guardian of the harem. Without warning it rushed at the ship and struck such a savage blow with its head that part of the keel broke away. Then the enraged whale swam away, only to return and attack again. This time it struck the starboard bow with its head. The planks caved in, and the crew on board barely had time to leap into the remaining small boats before the ship filled with water and fell over on her side. A few minutes later she sank.

Such was the magnificent, terrifying — and intelligent — animal that men began to hunt systematically around the oceans of the world some 200 years ago. At that time there were an estimated 600,000 sperm whales in the sea. Today there are possibly one-third that number, and at the present rate of destruction, and giving consideration to the modern weapons available for the task, it should not be long before they too, like the more vulnerable baleens, have been brought to the point of extinction.

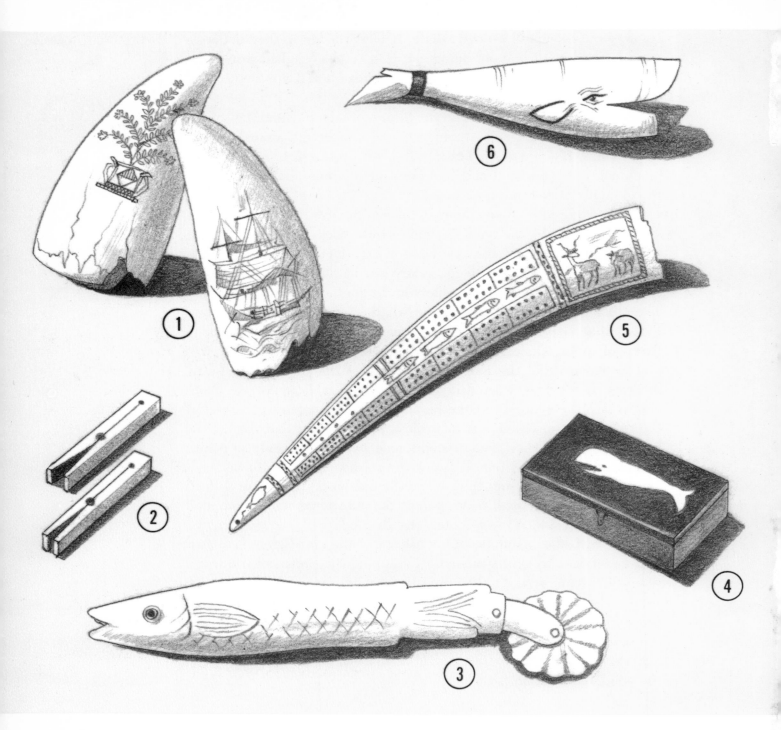

Scrimshaw: 1. Sperm whale teeth (carved) 2. Clothespins 3. Carved jagger for crimping (sperm whale jaw) 4. Jewel box inlaid 5. Scribbage board (walrus tusk) 6. Whale tooth (carved)

# 12
# Of Whalers
# and Whaling

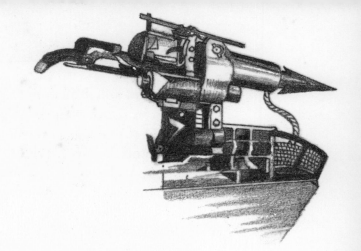

No BOOK about sea mammals would be complete without some mention of early whalers and the long history of whaling. For at least 5,000 years men have hunted various cetaceans. Cave paintings in northern Norway dating from at least 2000 B.C. show men in small boats pursuing porpoises. Stone harpoon heads of an even earlier date have been found in the same region. About 3000 B.C. the people of Crete were hunting dolphins in the eastern Mediterranean Sea, and by 1000 B.C. the Phoenicians had established a whaling industry around the port of Joppa, taking both right and sperm whales. It was there, in all probability, that the story of Jonah first was told.

Two thousand years later, during the tenth and eleventh centuries A.D., the Basques, a people of northeastern Spain and southwestern France, became Europe's leading whalers. Several whaling terms, such as the word "harpoon," come from the Basque language.

At first the Basques dealt only in stranded specimens. When an animal arrived on the beach, they flensed it, placed the blubber in pots on the shore, and boiled the contents to extract the oil. Afterward they sold the animal's baleen and either used the oil for lighting and heating or sold it too. If the stranded whale was still fresh enough, they ate all of the meat, except for the tongue. This portion was considered a great delicacy and was universally recognized as the property of the church.

Eventually these windfalls led to more organized procedures. Stone watchtowers were erected along the coast and were manned at all times during the winter and spring, when the Biscay right whales appeared on their annual migrations. As soon as the lookouts saw a whale spouting, bells were rung and piles of wet straw were lit, their smoky fires alerting the nearby villages. The men and boys then launched small wooden boats and rowed out a short distance beyond the breakers to reach their quarry. Shouting and making as much disturbance as possible, they drove the frightened right whales toward shore and killed them in shallow water with lances. Other species, like the even larger rorquals, were seen but not hunted because they were too fast to overtake and would sink immediately after death.

In time the Biscay right whales either were reduced in numbers or else grew chary of the waters close to shore, so that to hunt them on the open sea the Basques had to build larger and more seaworthy boats. By the 1500's the Basques were sailing their caravels across the Atlantic Ocean to Newfoundland, where they not only killed whales but also caught and salted great numbers of cod for their European customers. A Basque caravel was about 50 feet long and weighed 1,000 tons. At the top of the mizzenmast there was a crow's nest, 80 feet above the deck, where the watcher stood and looked for spouting whales.

The Basques also learned to hunt the Greenland right whale in the Arctic Ocean. At first they towed the dead animals to a convenient beach, where they flensed them and boiled the blubber in pots. But by the end of the 1500's their methods had changed, and the dead whales were boiled aboard ship. This was a time-saving operation, but also a risky one, for the pots stood over a furnace of bricks and there was always the chance that the flames, or some carelessly spilled oil, would cause a disastrous shipboard fire.

During these years no severe damage was done to the world's whale population. From 1517 until a century later a total of only 700 to 1,000 whales were killed by all of the Basque whaling ships—a far smaller number, indeed, than the 30,000 animals slaughtered *annually* in modern times.

Then in the 1600's the Dutch and English entered the whaling business. Sometimes their ships fought in the Arctic seas as the two nations competed for the valuable oil and baleen of the Greenland right whales. By 1621 the Dutch had fifty-two ships in the Arctic, each carrying a number of experienced Basque harpooners and flensers. The Dutch built shore stations, where the whales could be stripped and boiled. One such place, on the island of Spitsbergen, grew into a small, bustling town with an appropriate name. It was called Smeerenburg, which meant "Blubbertown."

During the 1700's and 1800's the British and Dutch killed off most of the Biscay and Greenland right whales in the Northern Hemisphere. The two species have never recovered from that early slaughter. Even today they are thought to number no more than a few hundred and are considered close to extinction.

114

Halfway around the world, the Japanese hunted whales too. At first they stayed in waters close to shore, but after a time they became more adept and eventually were able to kill California gray, sperm, and right whales on the open sea and even some of the faster-swimming rorquals, like the humpback.

Below the equator, the first white settlers in New Zealand and Australia began to take notice of the huge numbers of whales which regularly passed along the coasts. Soon that part of the world became the center of a new whaling industry. The southern right whale yielded a very valuable kind of oil, and toward the end of the 1700's the animals began to be killed by the thousands. British, American, and French whalers participated in the trade, which was not an especially easy one. More than one sailor was maimed or killed while hunting the animals. Occasionally, too, a sailor came to grief in a different way. The Maori people in New Zealand still practiced cannibalism, and from time to time an unlucky whaleman ended up as the feature item on the local menu. By the end of the 1820's the southern right whales started to grow scarce, and thirty years later so few were left that hunting in the area drew to a close.

Whaling in North America had begun centuries before, the Indians of New England having hunted the humpback and the right whales in shallow coastal waters, while some west coast tribes were hunting the California gray whale in the bays of Baja California. When the Pilgrims reached New England, they first learned about whaling from the Indians. The local tribes used fleets of bark canoes. Their weapons were harpoons with sharp, bone-head points and flights of arrows, which they shot into a harpooned animal.

For a time the white settlers and the Indians shared the toil and the profits. Then on Nantucket Island and along the New England coast the settlers built small whaling ships and began to make brief but profitable hunting trips beyond the sight of land.

In 1712, while seeking right whales, Captain Christopher Hussey managed to kill a sperm whale, flensed it at sea, and brought the valuable spermaceti and oil back to port. As the right whales were already becoming noticeably fewer, Captain Hussey's success encouraged the more enterprising New England whalers to build larger ships in order to pursue the more wide-ranging sperm whale across the open ocean. Before long the American sperm whale industry was beginning to flourish. By 1755 a sperm oil factory had been built in New Bedford, Massachusetts, and twenty years later sixty ocean-going sailing ships left the town each year to journey several thousand miles, sometimes as far as Cape Horn, in search of the sperm whale.

After the American Revolution, the sperm whale industry continued to prosper, despite several slack spells, for almost eighty years longer. During the nineteenth century American ships roamed through every quarter of the world in search of sperm whales, and it was said that no one could sail in the Indian Ocean for an entire day without meeting at least one Yankee whaler.

In 1846 the industry reached its zenith. Seventy thousand sailors were employed that year in 729 American sperm whalers. The profits for the shipowners were immense. One ship, the *Lagoda*, was built at a cost of $500 and within a dozen years had repaid its owner a total of $652,000.

The lowly whalemen, however, scarcely profited at all. According to one calculation, an average crew member received as his share of the enterprise after a three-year cruise the princely sum of $65 — less whatever clothing and tobacco he had purchased, usually at inflated prices, during the voyage. And if he had been charged with insubordination while at sea or some other infraction of shipboard rules, the mildest penalty was likely to be the complete loss of his share.

The officers' quarters on a whaler were comfortable enough, and the captain's cabin was even roomier, sometimes including a double bed, for often the captain brought along his wife. The crews' quarters were small, crowded, and not infrequently infested with rats and other vermin. A small oil lamp provided what little light there was, and a smoky oil stove provided heat. The work of harpooning and then killing a huge, enraged animal naturally was dangerous, and injuries and death were far from unknown. After the dead animal had been secured, the filthy job of flensing and boiling had to be done. The men endured this hard and ugly work as best they could, and between sightings they also had to endure stretches of intolerable boredom.

To help pass the tedious days American sailors carved and engraved the teeth and jawbones of sperm whales, practicing a kind of primitive art that became known as scrimshaw. The first step in making a piece of scrimshaw was to file down the ivory tooth or jaw until it was smooth. Then a design or picture was etched by a sharp instrument, like a sailmaker's needle. Finally soot, paint, or tar was rubbed into the scratched lines to bring out the design. The ivory scrimshaw was made into forks and spoons, napkin rings, decorative combs, cane heads, letter openers, and the jagged wheels once used for crimping pie crusts. Today many examples of the whalers' art are of considerable value and have been collected by private individuals and museums.

By the middle of the nineteenth century the sperm, California gray, and right whales had become so scarce that European and American whalers turned to smaller cetaceans, like the pilot whale, the narwhal, and the beluga. These animals, though, yielded comparatively little oil. In the meantime the fast-swimming rorquals still were not hunted, for they were almost impossible to catch in a sailing ship, and even when killed, they sank immediately.

As soon as steam replaced sail, the speed of the rorquals no longer was of consequence. But the animals still were not hunted because hand harpoons could not be thrown successfully from the deck of a pursuing ship. Then just over a century ago, in 1868, a Norwegian named Svend Foyn invented the harpoon gun. That year marked the beginning of modern whaling and the destruction of most of the world's remaining whales.

Soon compressed air began to be used to keep the slaughtered animals afloat. Year after year fleets of steam-powered whalers carrying harpoon guns roamed the seas, killed the fleeing rorquals, and then returned to shore, where the animals were cut up and disposed of. Whaling stations were built around the Northern Hemisphere, but the harpoon gun was so effective that by 1910 there was scarcely any whaling left above the equator.

The eyes of the whalers then turned to the remote regions of Antarctica. The first southern whaling station was built in 1904. In a short time a new and fearful slaughter had begun, with much of the shore activity centered on the wretched island of South Georgia. In the 1920's and 1930's the last refinement was made: Truly modern factory ships were developed that treated the animals on board, so that the whalers did not have to waste time returning to port during the hunting season.

In 1923 a single mother ship, accompanied by five scouting-and-killing ships, called catchers, went to the Ross Sea. It returned with 17,500 barrels of whale oil. In the following two years it took 32,000 and 40,000 barrels. By 1934 the Antarctic slaughter had grown to gigantic proportions. That year more than 30,000 whales were killed. One current estimate is that since 1900 more than 800,000 cetaceans have been killed, mostly in the Southern Hemisphere, for their oil, spermaceti, meat, and baleen.

In the Antarctic, the last region where whales existed in large numbers even a few years ago, there was no escape for the hunted animals. As recently as 1940 there might have been some 40,000 to 50,000 blue whales left, as well as 200,000 to 250,000 fin whales and 20,000 humpbacks. By the late 1950's these numbers had been reduced to less than 10,000 blues, 40,000 fins, and about 1,600 humpbacks. Today blue whales number less than 1,000 and the other species also have declined sharply.

For many centuries baleen and whale oil were unique. But today plastics and other materials with the same properties as baleen can be produced in any chemical laboratory, and whale oil is hardly needed now to light the reading lamps of the world. And though it may cost a little more, surely an ingenious nation like Japan could find an alternative source of protein for its people, instead of plundering, for meat and poultry feed, our planet's last few herds of giant whales.

More than two decades ago the International Whaling Commission was formed. Its attempts to control commercial whaling and to prevent the final destruction of the oceans' largest sea mammals have thus far been a failure. At present the Japanese and Russians are the chief culprits. Neither nation abides by the rules of the commission; neither nation will limit its catch. Between them they still destroy 20,000 whales each year and show no signs of changing their ways. Perhaps a worldwide outcry directed from the heads of other governments might bring an end to the killing before all of the animals are gone — but then, even that action might very well fail, for the whales are in desperate straits.

The problem of greedy men and helpless sea animals is not a new one. It was recognized more than a century ago by Herman Melville, who wrote in *Moby Dick*:

Whether owing to the omniscient look-outs at the mastheads of the whale-ships . . . and the thousand harpoons and lances darted along all the continental coasts; the moot point is, whether Leviathan can long endure so wide a chase, and so remorseless a havoc; whether he must not at last be exterminated from the waters.

Today it would seem that leviathan is not likely to endure much longer. And if that should happen, and he should finally disappear, any thinking person will know at once that the world in which we all must live has become a poorer place because of it.

# Bibliography

Augusta, Josef, *The Age of Monsters*. London, Paul Hamlyn, Ltd., 1966. Contains a short description of Dr. Albert Koch and his notorious "sea serpent."

Bennett, Frederick, *Narrative of a Whaling Voyage*. London, Richard Bentley, 1840. Unusual nineteenth-century account of whalers and whaling. For advanced readers.

Bridges, William, *New York Aquarium Book of the Water World*. New York, American Heritage Press, 1970. Mainly devoted to fishes, but with interesting material on sea mammals as well.

Carrington, Richard, *Mermaids and Mastodons*. London, Arrow Books, 1960. Amusing and informative material on kraken, mermaids, etc.

Caulfield, Patricia, *Everglades*. New York, Sierra Club/Ballantine Books, 1971. Brief mention of American manatee. Beautiful photographs.

Chase, Owen, *Account of the Essex Disaster*. Various. Description of famous early-nineteenth-century whaling voyage, which served as a partial model for Melville's later masterpiece.

Giambara, Paul, *Whales, Whaling, and Whalecraft*. Centerville, Massachusetts, Scrimshaw Publishing, 1967. One of many general titles on whaling.

*King, Judith E., *Seals of the World*. London, The British Museum, 1964. Expert descriptions of various pinnipeds. Invaluable material for advanced students.

Lilly, John C., *Man and Dolphin*. New York, Pyramid Books, 1969. Study of the bottlenosed dolphin. Emphasis on interspecies communication. For advanced students.

———, *The Mind of the Dolphin*. New York, Avon Books, 1969. Further study of *Tursiops truncatus*.

Melville, Herman, *Moby Dick*. Various. American fiction classic. Unmatched whaling descriptions.

*Ommanney, F. D., *Lost Leviathan*. New York, Dodd, Mead, 1971. Current and choice. Highly readable. Expert material on many phases of whales and whaling.

Porter, Eliot, *Galapagos*. New York, Sierra Club/Ballantine Books, 1971. Some interesting but limited material about seals in the islands made famous by Charles Darwin. Brilliant photographs.

*Robertson, R. B., *Of Whales and Men*. New York, Knopf, 1954. Fine work on modern whaling and whaling men in the Antarctic. For advanced readers.

Robotti, Frances D., *Whaling and Old Salem*. New York, Bonanza Books, 1962. Interesting tales of American whalers.

Sanderson, Ivan T., *Living Mammals of the World*. New York, Doubleday, 1965. Interesting material on marine mammals. A few good photographs.

*Scammon, Charles M., *The Marine Mammals of the Northwestern Coast of North America*. New York, Dover, 1968. Reissue of a unique nineteenth-century whaling and sealing classic long out of print. Many firsthand descriptions of sealing and whaling methods employed by America's seamen along the coasts of California and Alaska. A number of brilliant etchings, not always accurate, but always fascinating.

Scheele, William E., *The First Mammals*. Cleveland and New York, World, 1955. Includes brief mention of manatee and *Zeuglodon*.

*Scheffer, Victor B., *The Year of the Seal*.

* Particularly useful or important titles.

119

New York, Scribner's, 1970. Invaluable material about the Alaska fur seal, much of it gathered firsthand on the distant Pribilof Islands. Author a highly gifted naturalist.

*———, *The Year of the Whale*. New York, Scribner's, 1969. Few contemporary nature writers can match the author for style and content.

*STUART, FRANK S., *A Seal's World*. New York, Pyramid Books, 1967. Fascinating account of seal's life. Factual basis for highly readable fictional narrative.

*WALKER, ERNEST P., ed., *Mammals of the World*, 2d ed. Baltimore, Md., Johns Hopkins Press, 1968 3 vols. Extensive and invaluable material on all sea mammals. For advanced students. Interesting photographs.

Valuable articles are to be found in recent issues of the following periodicals and newspapers:
*National Geographic*
*Natural History*
New York *Times*
*\*Smithsonian* magazine
*Sports Illustrated*
U.S. Department of the Interior Circulars

* Particularly useful or important titles.

Giant
bottle-nosed whale
(*Berardius bairdi*)

# Classification of Vertebrate Sea Animals

Class Pisces (fish)
Class Amphibia (frogs, salamanders, toads)
Class Reptilia (crocodiles, lizards, snakes, turtles)
Class Aves (birds)

Class Mammalia (warm-blooded, fur-bearing vertebrates; included among them are four animal orders,
Sirenia, Carnivora, Pinnipedia, and Cetacea, each of which contains at least one species of sea mammal.

Order Sirenia—Consists of just two families:
the dugongs and the manatees.
Dugongs, family Dugongidae:
Steller's sea cow, *Hydrodamalis stelleri*. Sometimes called the giant sea cow. Now extinct.
Dugong, *Dugong dugon*. The only living species of dugong.
Manatees, family Trichechidae:
American manatee, *Trichechus manatus*. Sighted occasionally in the Everglades. Has even been reported within the city limits of Miami.
South American or Amazonian manatee, *Trichechus inunguis*. Lives in the freshwater tributaries of the Amazon and Orinoco rivers.
African manatee, *Trichechus senegalensis*. Mainly a sea dweller but also enters brackish and fresh water.

Order Carnivora—Includes, among others, such well-known families as the Canidae (dogs), the Ursidae (bears), the Felidae (cats), and the Mustelidae (weasels).
Weasels, family Mustelidae:

Sea otter, *Enhydra lutris*. This single species is the only sea mammal that belongs to the order Carnivora.

Order Pinnipedia—Consists of three principal family groups:
(1) the sea lions and fur seals; (2) the walruses; and (3) the true seals. The true seals include the elephant seals and the bladdernose seal.

("Walking" Pinnipeds)
Sea Lions, family Otariidae:
(*Species inhabiting the Northern Hemisphere*)
Northern, or Steller's, sea lion, *Eumetopias jubatus*. Probably the heaviest of all sea lions. Belligerent. Not suitable for circus training.
Californian sea lion, *Zalophus californianus*. Pinniped seen in zoos and circuses. Often misnamed "trained seal."
(*Species inhabiting the Southern Hemisphere*)
South American sea lion, *Otaria byronia*. Most numerous of the southern sea lions.
Australian sea lion, *Neophoca cinerea*. A large animal found only along the southern coast of Australia.
Hooker's sea lion, *Phocarctos hookeri*. A victim of nineteenth-century sealers. Still scarce today.

Fur seals, family Otariidae:
(*Species inhabiting the Northern Hemisphere*)
Alaska, northern, or Pribilof fur seal, *Callorhinus ursinus*. The subject of much current study and contro-

versy. Possesses a very luxurious fur. (*Species inhabiting the Southern Hemisphere*)

South American fur seal, *Arctocephalus australis*. The greatest traveler among southern fur seals.

South African fur seal, *Arctocephalus pusillus*. More than 500,000 animals are now living off the African coast. In previous centuries twice hunted to near extinction.

Kerguelen fur seal, *Arctocephalus tropicalis*. Highest quality fur of any southern species. Formerly killed in great numbers. Now rare and fully protected.

Australian fur seal, *Arctocephalus doriferus*. One of three little-known species found in the area of New Zealand and Australia.

Tasmanian fur seal, *Arctocephalus tasmanicus*. A mystery animal. Few specimens have been studied.

New Zealand fur seal, *Arctocephalus forsteri*. Fifty thousand animals remain under government protection. Killed during the eighteenth and nineteenth centuries in huge numbers.

Guadalupe fur seal, *Arctocephalus philippii*. No longer found in Southern Hemisphere. Last herd of 300 or 400 animals now lives on Guadalupe Island, off the coast of Baja California.

Walruses, family Odobenidae:

Walrus, *Odobenus rosmarus*. Perhaps the most affectionate of all sea mammals. Long hunted for its ivory tusks, the walrus is declining in numbers year after year.

("Crawling" Pinnipeds)

Seals, family Phocidae:

(*Seals of the Northern Hemisphere*)

Harbor, common, spotted, or hair seal, *Phoca vitulina*. A coastal animal. Often mistaken during earlier times for a mermaid or siren.

Gray, or Atlantic, seal, *Halichoerus grypus*. Adults reach a length of 10 feet. These wide-ranging travelers have been sighted as far south as Atlantic City, New Jersey.

Greenland, or harp, seal, *Pagophilus groenlandicus*. Currently much in the news. The newborn pups are slaughtered in great numbers for their fur.

Bearded seal, *Erignathus barbatus*. An unsociable animal that whistles to its pups while underwater.

Ringed seal, *Pusa hispida*. Among the smallest of the pinnipeds, the ringed seal is of great importance to the Eskimos.

Caspian seal, *Pusa caspica*. This animal is found only in the Caspian Sea. Herds apparently are flourishing.

Baikal seal, *Pusa sibirica*. The Russians have disclosed little about this animal, which dwells in Lake Baikal, the deepest body of fresh water in the world.

Banded, or ribbon, seal, *Histriophoca fasciata*. A rare animal with curious markings. A few are killed annually by the Eskimos and converted into leather, oil, glue, and fertilizer.

(*Seals found in the Temperate Zone*)

West Indian monk seal, *Monachus tropicalis*. Christopher Columbus found these animals in great numbers on his second voyage to the Americas. None have been seen since 1952. Believed to be extinct.

Mediterranean monk seal, *Monachus monachus*. A very rare animal. Perhaps 5,000 still live in the Mediterranean Sea.

Hawaiian monk seal, *Monachus schauinslandi*. Almost extinct. Less than 2,000 animals thought to survive.

(*Seals of the Southern Hemisphere*)

Weddell seal, *Leptonychotes weddelli*. Half a million of these formidable divers are thought to inhabit the Antarctic. One specimen reached a depth of 1,800 feet.

Crabeater seal, *Lobodon carcinophagus*. There are between 2,000,000 and 5,000,000 of these swift animals living on the outer edge of the southern ice pack.

Leopard seal, *Hydrurga leptonyx.* The only seal to prey almost exclusively on warm-blooded creatures. Eats penguins and other seals.

Ross seal, *Ommatophoca rossi.* A rarely seen animal, noted for its bulging eyes and the cooing noises it makes occasionally.

(*The Bladdernose and Elephant Seals*)

Hooded, or bladdernose, seal, *Cystophora cristata.* A strange-looking pinniped. What purpose is served by the animal's remarkable nose bladder is not yet known.

Southern elephant seal, *Mirounga leonina.* The largest animal in the order Pinnipedia. Males grow to 20 feet and weigh up to 6,000 pounds.

Northern elephant seal, *Mirounga angustirostris.* Now a rare animal, numbering some 20,000. Once widely distributed, it is found only in the Temperate Zone, where it is protected by the United States and Mexican governments.

Order Cetacea—Consists of eight main families and some ninety species, including various whales, porpoises, and dolphins. Among the most interesting and important species are the following:

(Toothed Whales, Suborder Odontoceti)

Fresh water, or river, dolphins, family Platanistidae:

La Plata River dolphin, *Stenodelphis blainvillii.* A South American variety. Armed with more than 200 teeth for seizing and holding small fish.

Chinese dolphin, *Lipotes vexillifer.* An unusual animal found only in a single lake in China's Yangtze River.

Amazon dolphin, *Inia geoffrensis.*

Two specimens of this little-known animal were kept for a time and studied at the Fort Worth, Texas, zoo.

Beaked whales and bottle-nosed whales, family Ziphiidae:

Cuvier's beaked whale, *Ziphius cavirostris.* A medium-sized cetacean, reaching 25 feet in length. Found in all the world's oceans.

Giant bottle-nosed whale, *Berardius bairdi.* One of the largest of the porpoises. A wary animal, difficult to capture.

Belugas and Narwhals, family Monodontidae:

Beluga, or white, whale, *Delphinapterus leucas.* The strange "sea canary." Turns from black to white as it ages.

Narwhal, *Monodon monoceros.* An Arctic animal that possesses an odd-looking spiral tusk. In all probability the tusk serves no useful purpose.

Dolphins and porpoises, family Delphinidae:

Common dolphin, *Delphinus delphis.* A rapid swimmer, capable of twenty knots or more.

Pilot whale, or blackfish, *Globicephala melaena.* Often lives in schools of 500 to 700 animals. Has an innate tendency to "follow the leader." As a result, an entire school may become stranded on the beach.

Bottle-nosed dolphin, *Tursiops truncatus.* Trained and exhibited in public aquariums and outdoor "marineland" parks. A highly intelligent animal which remains the object of much scientific research.

Killer whale, *Orcinus orca.* An awesome marine predator. Diet includes seals, penguins, other whales, and sea otters. Specimens recently captured off the Pacific coast of North America proved docile in captivity.

Sperm whales, family Physeteridae:

Sperm whale, or cachalot, *Physeter catodon.* The Biblical animal that swallowed Jonah. Also the model for Herman Melville's immortal Moby Dick. Full-grown sperm whales reach 60 feet. Slaughtered in great numbers by American whalers during the nineteenth century.

(Baleen, or Toothless, Whales, Suborder Mysticeti)

Gray whales, family Eschrichtidae:

California gray whale, *Eschrichtius glaucus*. There are two separate populations, both greatly reduced, of this playful 40-foot animal. Ruthlessly decimated during the nineteenth century by American whalers.

Right whales, family Balaenidae:

Bowhead, or Greenland, right whale, *Balaena mysticetus*. A truly grotesque-looking animal. Once observed in large numbers as far south as Newfoundland. Now almost extinct.

Biscay, or black, right whale, *Eubalaena glacialis*. Now thought to number only 1,000 animals. Once highly prized for its oil and whalebone.

Pygmy right whale, *Caperea margi-*

*nata*. Smallest of its family. Always a rare animal. No more than thirty or forty specimens ever examined.

Rorquals, family Balaenopteridae:

Humpback whale, *Megaptera novaeangliae*. Another "playful" giant that enjoys cavorting in the water. Its voice has been studied, and some of its "songs" have been put on a long-playing record.

Sei whale, *Balaenoptera borealis*. The Japanese call it the sardine whale, because of its diet. Population reduced by half, to 75,000, during the past few years.

Fin whale, *Balaenoptera physalus*. A gregarious 80-foot giant which travels in large herds. World population recently reduced by 75 percent.

Blue, or sulphur-bottom, whale, *Sibbaldus musculus*. The largest animal that ever lived on earth. Can weigh as much as 125 tons, with a length of 100 to 120 feet. Numerous fifty years ago. Perhaps 1,000 animals now left—too few, some scientists believe, for the animal's survival.

Humpback whale
(*Megaptera
novaeangliae*)

# Index

Left, Red abalone (*Haliotis rufescens*)
Right, Pink abalone (*Haliotis corrugata*)

Archaeopteryx

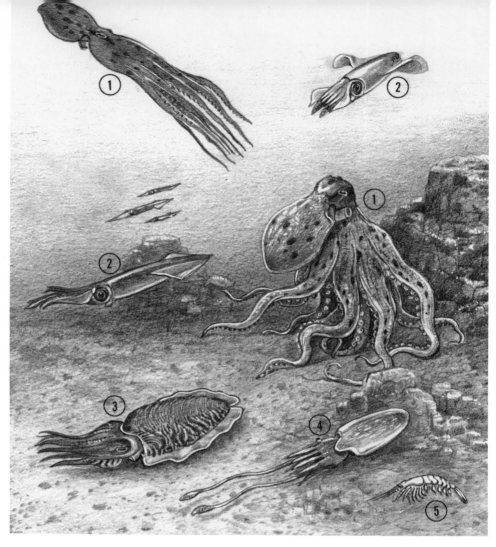

Leopard seal (*Hydrurga leptonyx*). Preys on Adélie penguin.

Food for whales and seals
1. Octopus (*Octopus vulgaris*)
2. American squid (*Loligo pealii*)
3. Common cuttlefish (*Sepa officinalis*)
4. Rare cuttlefish (*Sepia elegans*)
5. Krill (Shrimp) (Euphausid)

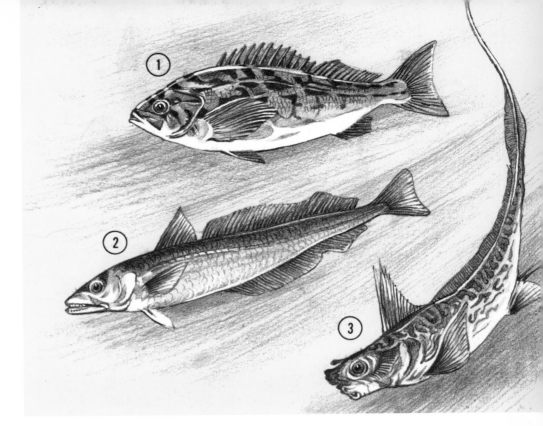

Food for Californian sea lions
1. Black rockfish (*Sebastodes mystinus*)
2. Hake (*Merluccius bilinearis*)
3. Ratfish (*Chimaera monstrosa*)

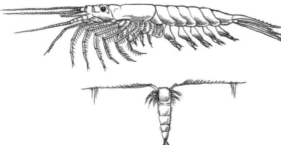

Krill (greatly magnified). Food for whales.
Upper, sea butterfly (*Euphausia superba*)
Lower, water flea (*Calanus sp.*)

Four classes of reptiles
1. Crocodiles. 2. Snakes. 3. Turtles. 4. Lizards

## The Author

WILLIAM WISE is the author of more than three dozen books and has earned several distinguished prizes for his writing. Three of his books have been Junior Literary Guild selections and one, *The Two Reigns of Tutankhamen*, received a Junior Book Award Medal from the Boys' Clubs of America. A versatile writer, Mr. Wise is the author of *Killer Smog*, one of the earliest books to warn adult readers of the world's air pollution crisis. More than twenty of his books have been published by Putnam, including biographies, books about exciting creatures of fact and fiction, and fanciful stories for young children.

## The Illustrator

JOSEPH SIBAL is a natural history artist whose paintings have illustrated semitechnical publications issued by museums. His paintings have also been reproduced in popular magazines, such as *Life*, and displayed in the Special Exhibit Gallery of the Bronx Zoo. For Putnam's, Mr. Sibal has also illustrated *Monsters of the Ancient Seas*, *The Strange World of Dinosaurs*, *The Strange World of Reptiles*, *The Strange World of Insects*, *The Amazing Animals of Latin America*, and *The Amazing Animals of Australia*.